Iron Age Artefacts in Wales

An investigation into the material culture of south-east Wales during the Pre-Roman Iron Age

Caroline Martin

BAR British Series 353
2003

Published in 2019 by
BAR Publishing, Oxford

BAR British Series 353

Iron Age Artefacts in Wales

ISBN 9781841713373 paperback
ISBN 9781407319940 e-book

DOI https://doi.org/10.30861/9781841713373

A catalogue record for this book is available from the British Library

This book is available at www.barpublishing.com

BAR Publishing is the trading name of British Archaeological Reports (Oxford) Ltd.
British Archaeological Reports was first incorporated in 1974 to publish the BAR
Series, International and British. In 1992 Hadrian Books Ltd became part of the BAR
group. This volume was originally published by John and Erica Hedges in conjunction
with British Archaeological Reports (Oxford) Ltd / Hadrian Books Ltd, the Series
principal publisher, in 2003. This present volume is published by BAR Publishing,
2019.

BAR
PUBLISHING

BAR titles are available from:

BAR Publishing
122 Banbury Rd, Oxford, OX2 7BP, UK
EMAIL   info@barpublishing.com
PHONE   +44 (0)1865 310431
FAX   +44 (0)1865 316916
www.barpublishing.com

Contents

Abstract

An investigation into the material culture of south-east Wales During the Pre-Roman Iron Age

The disparate and often fragmentary nature of artefacts from Iron Age Wales, in general, has created the impression that the archaeological record for this region of Britain is impoverished. This book will challenge that assumption and show that through the collection and collation of material culture recovered from a variety of contexts; including chance finds, hoard groups and those from excavations, a different picture emerges.

Whilst the information presented in this book has only been collected from two regions of Wales it offers a new interpretation of the variety and variability of artefacts available for further study in Wales as a whole for the Iron Age period.

Whilst the material culture available to date may not be vast in its quantities, what is available is often of a very high standard, illustrating that Wales at this period was not the backwater that it is often believed to have been but had contacts and associations with the rest of Europe.

The purpose of compiling this information about artefacts in south-east Wales was to demonstrate, that through the collection and collation of disparate and fragmentary information just how much material culture is available in a relatively small area and how much potential there is in this information for further research.

To contact me email: cmart3@tinyworld.co.uk

Acknowledgements

The contents of this volume consist of a postgraduate thesis I submitted to the University of Cardiff in 2002. There are two people without whose help I would never have finished the original paper. The first is Adam Gwilt at the National Museum and Gallery of Wales Cardiff whose kindness and patience far out ways his knowledge of the material culture he watches over (and that's saying something), I thank him very much for all his guidance, advise and help. The second is Ginny Nielsen who has helped me with my English and vocabulary on many, many, many occasions, and without her valued help my writing appears as double Dutch so thanks luv.

Thanks are also offered to Ginny's Danish husband Torben whose comprehension of the English language astounds me, to the ladies in the Arts and Humanities Library who are the un-sung heroines of Cardiff University thanks ladies, and to Dr Niall Sharples for reading a number of my chapters, to Dr Ray Howell and Dr Joshua Pollard at UWCN for allowing me to use the picture of the La Téne brooch recovered from the Lodge Hill excavations and Kate Smith a big thanks and woof for taking time out of your busy doctoral schedule to help edit this book and finally to my husband Kevin who has supported me throughout this marathon, love always.

"Take heed: you do not find what you do not seek."

English Proverb (Unprovenanced)

Figures

Tables

Chapter 1

Introductory Remarks & Methodology

My interest in the Iron Age was sparked by my undergraduate dissertation in which I conducted a study of the hillforts of south-east Wales. Whilst searching the literature for information on aspects of the Iron Age in Wales it became clear how disparate and fragmentary information was regarding Welsh artefacts. I, therefore, decided to investigate what artefacts were available for study throughout Wales.

Aims of research

The main aims and objectives of this study are to:

Collect and present fragmentary information via the creation of a database;

Introduce the quantity and quality of material culture available for south-east Wales from the Iron Age period;

Establish the potential for further research.

Background to the research

In order to establish the range of artefacts most suitable for incorporation within this investigation, a pilot study was set up. This highlighted the practicality of narrowing the scope of the study, which was to include data from the whole of Wales. Material culture and related literature was therefore recovered from two counties in south-east Wales, namely, Gwent and Glamorgan, two of the pre-1974 county boundaries.

Details of the database

The database included as a glossary consists of lists of data retrieved from twenty-two excavated sites, four hoard groups and the remainder are from chance finds. Whilst every effort has been made to include all material culture from the study area, some sites and objects may have been overlooked.

Structure of work

Descriptions and information about each artefact is taken from a number of sources. The following abbreviations are applicable throughout this work and the original figure numbers for drawings or pictures have been retained from their original sources where applicable.

N.M.W: The National Museum and Gallery of Wales.

N.M.W.P.A: The Portable Antiquities Scheme.

N.P.T: Newport Museum.

S.W.S: Swansea Museum

N.G.R: National Grid Reference.

A.I.W: Archaeology in Wales.

D &S: Davies and Spratling (1976)

Unknown: Unknown repository and or unknown accession number.

Structure of chapters

Chapter 2 reviews literature concerning artefact studies concerned with the Iron Age in Britain in general.

Chapter 3 presents material culture collected from hoards recovered from south-east Wales.

Chapter 4 examines chance finds recovered in a variety of ways.

Chapter 5 will evaluate and discuss the artefacts recovered through excavation.

Chapter 6 discusses material culture presented and considers the important role the collection and collation of fragmentary data can play in the advancement of our understanding the archaeology of a specific region.

Structure of tables

Included throughout this work are a number of tables illustrating the number of different objects listed under a variety of headings. Each heading refers to a different group of artefacts. Below is a brief description of which objects will be included under each heading:

Adornment

Objects that can be worn on the body or used in personal care or cleaning of the body such as brooches, rings, bracelets, belt hooks, tweezers etc.

Animal Bones

Animal bones recovered from all contexts.

Burial

Human skeletal remains.

Coins

Coins of varying descriptions from the study area.

Consumption

Objects that can be associated with high status consumption of food or drink, such as cauldrons, tankards etc. but excluding ceramic vessels.

Domestic Production

Objects that may have been used or made in the home; items included are spindle whorls, querns stones, loom weights, pot boilers etc.

Horse

Objects that can be associated with military activity including horse and chariot/wagon fittings.

Pottery

Any Iron Age pottery recovered.

Production

Objects used in industrial/manufacturing processes; i.e. metalwork activity and production.

Religious

Objects thought to hold religious connotations.

Tools

Objects that may have been used in tending land or employed in everyday practices i.e. chopping wood, as well as objects that may have been used in the manufacture of items used in the home i.e. cloth or leather, etc.

Unknown

Objects of unknown description.

Weapons

Objects considered to be intended for use in combat

Wood

Objects made from wood.

Limitations of this work

Whilst important, this type of investigation has many limitations. The material under examination and the findings of this study are only applicable to the regions under discussion and are not indicative of the material cultural record for the whole of Wales. However, this study illustrates the importance of bringing together disparate fragments of information that have been neglected for decades in doing so, we can gain an important insight into the people that lived in south-east Wales during the Iron Age period and create a building block for further research.

Chapter 2

A Review of the Literature

Introduction

This chapter provides a brief overview of the studies of artefacts in the British Iron Age. It considers the great diversity of investigations into artefacts studies and reflects on the general lack of synthesis of their findings. Although this is not an exhaustive review of associated literature, it illustrates the great diversity of artefact studies in the British Iron Age.

Artefacts are objects that have been used, modified or made by people. They include the discarded refuse from the daily activities of human existence such as broken pottery, fragments of metal work, scraps of food or textiles; all of which leave tantalising traces of everyday life in antiquity (Renfrew & Bahn 1996: 45). The study of material culture provides information on many aspects of human activity, including production, technology, contact, exchange and site function (Haselgrove *et al* 2000). Haselgrove (1999) maintains that there are three levels of craft activity identifiable within the archaeological record during the Iron Age:

i.   Output to meet individual households or community needs

ii.   Specialised production for wider distribution

iii. Luxury goods for the wealthiest sections of society.

However, for the majority of material culture there is little evidence of the sites where they were produced the only tangible evidence we have are the artefacts themselves and these only hint at the scale and scope employed in the manufacture of objects (Haselgrove 1999:125). Craft production and exchange have dominated artefact-based research in Britain for the last three decades (Morris 1996: 41). In an attempt to understand how production was organised and exchanges made (Cunliffe 1984: 556-9) postulated that hillforts were redistribution centres where local surplus was accumulated and exchanged for extra-regional raw materials and that this process was organised and under the control of a ruling elite (Morris 1996: 41). Cunliffe's work at Danebury provided an impetus for important analysis (Hill 1995: 52). The excavation and retrieval of large quantities of artefactual, structural and organic data from sites such as Danebury (Cunliffe 1995), Gussage All Saints (Foster 1980; Wainwright & Spratling 1973) and Maiden Castle (Sharples 1991) has led to important research in many sections of artefact studies. However, whilst there have been improvements in may areas of this research we still lack a basic understanding of

technology, typology, distribution and dating of a large number of artefact groups (Haselgrove *et al* 2000).

Metal Work

Sites that have yielded evidence of iron working illustrate the potential for advancing present knowledge in the techniques and technology used in these activities. Excavations such as Llwyn Bryn-dinas (1989; Musson *et al* 1992) how we might identify how and where metal production was conducted. The study of metalworking in copper alloy (Musson *et al* 1992: 277-80), and iron (Crew 1984; 1998; 1991) has received a heightened profile in the past two decades especially in north Wales. The study of copper alloys has demonstrated the potential of analysis of other metals (Northover 1984; Dungworth 1996; Musson *et al* 1992: 279; Musson & Northover 1989: 15-26). The study of moulds and crucibles is well established (Foster 1980; Bayley 1992; Morris 1997), however, not so well established is the detailed technological examination of objects which is essential to understanding artefacts within their cultural contexts (Haselgrove *et al* 2000). Over the last twenty years increasing scientific analysis has resulted in important advances in our understanding of iron, bronze, silver and gold working (Warner 1993) during the British Iron Age (e.g., Ehrenreich 1994; Scott: 1991; Northover 1987; Dungworth 1996; Bayley 1998; Crew 1995). Bayley's research on metal work indicates how the gradual accumulation of data can produce excellent results (Haselgrove *et al* 2000: 22; Bayley 1998). Hingley's (1990) work illustrates the importance of studying individual artefact groups and shows how interpretations can be altered and new avenues of investigation opened through the investigation of deposition, location, and contexts of artefacts. Later work by Hingley (1997) on symbolic aspects of metalworking is a reminder that archaeologists have only a partial view and understanding of the amount of symbolism attached to iron working in the British Iron Age.

Metal Work and Art Styles

Numerous examples of 'Celtic' artwork in Britain are in print (Fox 1958; Jope 2000; Macgregor 1976; Megaw & Megaw 1989) and individual pieces of decorated metal work have received detailed analysis (Stead 1985; 1991; 1998; MacDonald 2000: Manning 1972). However, many categories of artefacts remain under-researched; these include pins (Dunning 1934) and more recently horse bits (Palk 1984) and strap unions (Taylor and Braisford 1985). swords (Piggott 1950), although Ian Stead is working on a corpus of Iron Age Swords at present.

Iron Age Hoards are a valuable source of archaeological information and are present in all areas of Britain, however, whilst some hoard groups have received individual attention, as yet there is no corpus available listing all of the major Iron Age hoards in Britain (MacDonald. 2000; Stead 1991; 1998; Savory 1964; Davies and Spratling 1976). Work conducted by Phillip MacDonald (2000) illustrated the importance of re-evaluating well-known assemblages. His re-analysis of the Llyn Cerrig Bach hoard greatly enhances our understanding of this well-known assemblage, setting a precedent for future research of this kind in Britain. Another important study conducted by Hunter (1997) includes hoard groups recovered from both Scotland and northern England. Investigations conducted by Taylor and Brailsford (1985), Piggott (1950) and Hull and Hawkes (1987) exemplify that the study of singular artefact groups can produce outstanding results in classification systems and chronologies.

Bodily Care and Ornamentation

Jackson (1985) and Hill (1997) highlight many aspects regarding bodily care and ornamentation during the Iron Age period. Jackson's work demonstrates that items employed in bodily care and ornamentation were distributed throughout Britain in the Late Iron Age, whilst Hill's work focuses more on the Romano-British period. Jackson's work is based on an article by R. A Smith (1918) entitled *A particular type of Roman bronze Pendent*, a paper that completely altered how the archaeological world viewed such objects. In conjunction with the theme of bodily care and ornamentation are the uses of prehistoric combs, made of bone and antler is also relevant to this (Tuohy 1999).

The study of glass and its use as inlay and decoration in a number of objects is well represented in the recorded material culture from the British Iron Age. Studies of glass beads have been carried out by Guido (1978) and Kilbridie-Jones (1938) and a study of glass bangles by Stevenson (1965; 1976). Whilst a good typological base is available, questions concerning the techniques used in glass manufacture remain unanswered. Enamel use and manufacture is a good case in point; the often brightly coloured enamels such as red and yellow, which are well represented in the archaeological record, have received little attention in recent years, however, a forthcoming paper is awaited by A Davis & A Gwilt. The corpus of pre-Roman brooches, by Hull and Hawkes (1987) whilst very important, requires updating to include recent discoveries (Haselgrove 1997; Haselgrove *et al* 2000: 17). Furthermore, the bulk of material in the corpus represents brooches found in southern England. An updated corpus expanded to include the other countries that make up Britain would be desirable. Haselgrove (1997) discusses the distribution and chronology of Iron Age brooches offering new insight into how, why and where brooches were being deposited.

Until recently it has been difficult to make a distinction between jet, (Beck and Shennan 1990) shale and cannel coal because of their structural and aesthetic similarities. Scientific tests conducted by scholars at both Cardiff University (Morris and Rowlands 1993) and the University of Bradford (Hunter, McDonnell and Pollard 1993) have established a technique that enables the differentiation of the various components of the materials under investigation to be recognised. Scientific analysis is invaluable in our understanding of what types of materials were being exploited and producing insight into the locations from which the materials were being extracted; this in turn can aid the interpretation of the exchange mechanisms that were in place during the Iron Age.

Ceramics

There are a variety of general reviews looking at ceramic research (Morris 1994) These already set priorities for research and established minimum standards for recording and publication. Others (Willis 1996; Rigby and Freestone; Gwilt 1997; Brown 1997) have considered technology, typology, distribution, use and meaning. A limited amount of work has been carried out on pottery, including decorated varieties, from the Northern and Western Isles (Topping 1987; Lane 1990; Campbell 1991). Recent work indicates how the detailed study of form, size and use of pottery can help us understand the ways in which food and liquids were stored, prepared and consumed in the Iron Age (Woodward 1997; Woodward and Blinkhorn 1997; Earwood 1991; 1993). The techniques employed in organic residue analysis have developed to the extent that useful questions can be tackled, however, the function of pottery still requires investigation (Dudd and Evershed 1998; Heron *et al* 1991). A substantial amount of work conducted by Elaine Morris on salt distribution and the containers used to transport it revealed the extent of its trade networks during the Iron Age (Morris 1985; 1994).

Summary

The collection of empirical data, often maligned (Haselgrove *et al* 2000), are imperative to archaeological research. The accumulation and sequential analysis of material culture can greatly enhance our understanding of typology, chronology and exchange patterns it can also change perceptions of how we view the uses and amounts of material culture visible in the archaeological record (Hallén 1994; Coles and Minnitt 1995: 137-79; Evans 1989). This brief review has illustrated some of the advances made in artefact studies in Britain. Whilst our understanding and awareness of the function, technologies and manufacture of many objects is progressing, clearly, there is scope for much further work to be done.

Chapter 3

Chance Finds

Introduction

Every year members of the public throughout Britain discover objects of archaeological importance. As many of the finds are made by metal detectorists, little of the material recovered is recorded by museums or archaeologists and therefore, a great deal of potential information is lost. In July 1996, the Treasure Act, which reformed the medieval common law of Treasure Trove, gained royal assent. Ultimately this led to a significant increase in the number of discoveries being reported in England and Wales, however, the majority of archaeological finds fall outside the scope of this act. Subsequently, the Government launched an initiative to promote the voluntary recording of archaeological finds. This initiative, The Portable Antiquities Recording Scheme, originally began as six pilot schemes in various parts of England during the latter part of 1997. This was followed by a second wave of pilot schemes, including one that extended to the whole of Wales and was funded by the Heritage Lottery Fund for a period of eighteen months. The pilot scheme for Wales initially ran from March 1999 to August 2000. Further funding was allocated by a number of bodies including The National Assembly for Wales, The Council for Museums, Archives and Libraries and a further grant from the Heritage Lottery Fund enabling the Welsh Scheme to continue (MacDonald 2000: 44). The people most responsible for reporting archaeological finds to the scheme are metal detectorists and whilst in the past relationships between archaeologists and metal detectorists have been fraught with difficulties, there have been important advances between these two groups since the scheme began. In addition to the artefacts recovered by metal detectorists, a significant number of finds are made by both amateur field walkers and other members of the public who discover objects whilst out walking or engaged in other leisure activities (MacDonald 2000: 45).

Although, The Portable Antiquities Scheme has only been running for a short period, the database is increasing rapidly. The establishment of this scheme has encouraged members of the public to take a more responsible attitude towards the archaeology and culture of Wales. Whilst there is an attitude amongst most members of the public supporting the preservation and display of all things archaeological and historical, there are still those who seek artefacts for monetary gain. As mentioned above relations between metal detectorists and the archaeological and historical worlds have improved greatly since the scheme's establishment, however, some metal detectorists are still wary of official bodies and refuse to join the scheme. I hope that further encouragement and persuasion by museum curators, archaeologists and historians will break down the barriers.

A note on the objects in the index

This chapter lists the objects that have been recovered as chance finds. These objects are so diverse that it was necessary to list them by category heading rather than individually. Discoveries are being made constantly, and as such this section may well be out of date before it is finished. For the most up to date additions to this ever expanding database consult 'The Portable Antiquities Scheme' which can be found at either The National Museum and Gallery of Wales, Cardiff or by logging onto their website at www.finds.org.uk/. Whilst every effort has been made to include all of, the chance finds from the study area, some may have been overlooked. For the most part, the number of artefacts recovered from any given area does not exceed one or two objects, however, in the case of Merthyr Mawr Warren over forty objects are recorded. Due to word limitation of this book, it would not be feasible to discuss them all, therefore, a brief description plus the museum accession number and any bibliographical references that are relevant to each object is included.

Index of chance finds

Adornment

Copper alloy casting, found outside the southern wall at Caerwent, Monmouthshire. The object consists of a short length of hoop; two narrow circular-sectioned conical terminals and seven graded beaded mouldings. The surface of this example is corroded and could be a section of a beaded neck-ring or beaded torc. Beaded torcs are two-part items made of a simple curved bar, usually circular or rectangular in section, and a shorter beaded section. The sections are then joined by means of mortise and tenon like joints on their terminals. The distribution of beaded torcs is normally restricted to the north of England and southern Scotland, although there are examples at Tre'r Ceiri in Caernarvonshire (Hughes 1907: 40-2, fig 2). Beaded torcs date to the 1st and 2nd centuries AD (MacGregor 1976: 98-9). This example is similar in form to one found at Sully in Glamorgan (MacDonald 99.96.1).
N.G.R: ST 470 903. N.M.W.P.A: 99.96.1.

Beads found at St Brides Major. Complete Iron Age glass beads and the damaged remains of another found within a couple of metres of each other. Both beads are examples of Guido's Group Class 6 or Oldbury type (Guido 1978: 53-7, 112-117, plates, 1.6 a-c, III.a). These are large beads of dark, almost opaque, blue glass decorated with nine trailed and marvered opaque yellow glass spirals. The damaged bead has been burnt or exposed to heat and is completely opaque, distorted and vitrified. Beads of the Oldbury type are concentrated in southern Britain during the last two centuries BC and the first century AD. Three Oldbury beads are known from Wales: one from the Breidden hillfort, Montgomeryshire (Guido 1978: 116; Musson, Britnell and Smith 1991:158, no 315, fig 65), one from Gronant, near Prestatyn, Flintshire (Guido 1978: 116) and one from Glanbidno-uchaf, near Llangurig, Gwynydd (Boon 1980:745, no 1, fig 1.1; MacDonald 1999: 94). N.G.R: SS 90 75.

Ring found at St Brides Major. This is a fragment of a nearly circular carved and polished cannel-coal ring found as a surface find in a ploughed field. This item was found in the same location as the glass beads. Only about a quarter of the ring remains, the inner edge of which is flat with rounded corners. A number of black lithic raw materials such as cannel coal; jet and shale were used for making jewellery and ornaments in antiquity. The function of the ring is uncertain; in section, it is similar to a late Iron Age armlet from a settlement site at Rope Lake Hole, Corfe Castle, Dorset (Cox and Woodward 1987: 28, fig 93). Dating of this object is uncertain due to the lack of archaeological research conducted upon cannel-coal artefact typologies, however, given the close proximity to

the two Iron Age glass beads and the similarity it shows to the Rope Lake Hole example, a Late Iron Age or early Roman date has been suggested (MacDonald and Davies 2000: 93-4). N.G.R: SS 90 75

Annular bead, Guido's group 5, found in Lower Machen, Gwent. N.G.R: ST 241 889. N.M.W.P.A: 2000.123.32.

A single complete small, undecorated blue glass annular bead was found at Hatterall Hill near Cymyoy in Monmouthshire and is of Guido's Group 6, subgroup ivb (Guido 1978: 66-8 and 155-62). Beads of this type were produced over a long period, mainly between 6th century BC and 8th century AD (Guido 1978: 68; Guido 1999: 48). In Wales, examples of this type of bead are mostly associated with sites of an Iron Age and Romano-British date. There is a well-dated parallel of this bead at Twyn y Gaer (Probert 1976) hillfort in Monmouthshire dating to between 3rd and 1st centuries BC and at Sudbrook (Nash-Williams 1939) hillfort in Monmouthshire dating to 1st centuries BC and AD. It has been suggested that these beads were manufactured at the Meare Lake Villages (Bulleid 1927), where evidence of glass bead production has been discovered (Henderson 1981: 1987). An Iron Age date has been tentatively applied to this bead but it also could fall within the parameters set out by Guido. N.G.R: SO 310 250. N.M.W.P.A: 2001:118.2.

Ring headed pin made of copper of Early Iron Age date this example was found at Margam Beach. N.G.R: SS 760 868. NM.W: 88.48.H1.

A La Tène 1 brooch was found on Newton Moor, Penllyn. This is an example of the 'Wessex' form of Type 1Ba La Tène I brooch (Hull and Hawkes 1987: 95). This example is relatively small and dates to the first half of the 4th century BC although there are some later survivals. The Newton Moor brooch is unusual in that the mock spring mechanism has been repaired from what appears to be a fragment from another object, giving the brooch a unilateral appearance. Although this feature is unusual in La Tène I brooches, it would not have prevented the brooch working as a clothes fastener. It has been suggested (MacDonald 2000:92) that the repair to the brooch's spring mechanism rather than being a functional repair is a poorly-executed non-functional repair, done for the purpose of giving the brooch the appearance of being complete prior to being offered as a votive deposition (Gwilt pers comm, MacDonald 2000: 91-2).
N.G.R: SS 98 75. A.I.W: 2000: 91-2. See figure 1.
Cast copper alloy mount of a raised boss, possible human head in form with a pointed chin and an integrally cast looped terminal found at New Mill Farm, Penhow. Most of

the original surface is lost but two sub-circular punched dots and a cast transverse groove give the impressions of eyes, a chin and a beard. The dating of the casting is consistent with a late Iron Age or early Romano-British attribution; a literature search by MacDonald did not produce any close parallels (MacDonald NMGWPA: 2000.69.1). N.G.R: ST 397 921. N.M.W.P.A: 2000.69.1.

Brooch found at Penllyn Moor, N.G.R: La Tène I Type I either Ba or IBb. (Hull and Hawkes 1987: 72-132). This example is incomplete and includes a plain arched bow, first coil of spring, part of the foot and the catch-plate. The diagnostic part of the brooch did not survive, the small stature of the brooch and the shape of the remaining coil suggests dates of the 4th century BC, although later survival of this type is known (Hull and Hawkes1987: 97; MacDonald 2000). N.G.R: SS 9828 7631. N.M.W.P.A: 2000.2.4.1.

Coins

An Iron Age potin coin was discovered in the mid 1990s at Lower Llanmelin. This potin is an example of the *la tète diabolique* type, which is part of the Butting-Bull series, traditionally attributed to the Turones of central Gaul (Allen 1995: 85. no 287ff). The Butting Bull series of potins almost certainly predates the Gallic War of the mid 1st century BC, but does not help indicate when this coin was imported into Britain. The coin could have been brought into Britain several decades after it was cast. Potins of this type are common in Gaul but very rare in Britain, a few are recorded on the southern coast of England and Kent. (Besly and MacDonald 2000: 76). N.G.R: ST 460 925. A.I.W: 2000.76.

Two coins recovered near Trelech. Both coins are 'Celtic' gold staters of the Dobunni tribe and were found in plough soil by a metal detectorist in the Trelech-Llanishen area in September 1998 and are dated from 30 BC (Bray, J. 1998: 100, 86). N.G.R: SO 48 04. A.I.W 1997: 100; A.I.W 1998: 86.

Dobunnic gold slater coin found at St Arvans, near Chepstow this coin is dated from 10 BC to AD 10 with an inscription that reads [ANTED RIG]. No N.G.R. N.P.T: 94.150.

Consumption

Cast copper alloy, 'human head' vessel mount found near Llanmelin, Monmouthshire. This object is lightly domed and is a roughly shield-shaped mount. Outer surface is decorated with incised decoration in the form of a human face with vertically dressed hair running down to the forehead, side-whiskers and strong eyebrows. MacDonald (1999) found it difficult to identify a date and function for this piece but suggests it may be of a late Iron Age or early Roman date (MacDonald: 99.79.1). N.G.R: ST 4580 9193. N.M.W.P.A: 99.79.1.

Horse

Cast copper alloy strap union found near Cowbridge in Glamorgan. This example consists of two conjoined and perforated sub-triangular loops that form a figure of eight and are flanked on either side by a vertical bar attached to each loop. The back is flat and the bars are slightly rounded in the cross section presumably through wear and tear. The surface is pitted and faint traces of simple curvilinear motifs are visible; these decorative motifs are paralleled by those on a strap union from Churchdown, Gloucestershire (Watkins 1985: 319-20). This is an example of Taylor's and Brailsford's Type I (1985: 247-253). The date range of Type I extends from the 1st century BC to the second half of the 1st century AD. Strap unions of this size are normally assumed to be harness fittings (Taylor and Brailsford 1985), however, it is more than probable that the smaller examples of strap union were used as human dress accessories (Watkins 1985: 319; Champion 1995: 418; MacDonald: 2001.45.1). N.G.R: ST 002 752. N.M.W.P.A: 2001.45.1.

Copper alloy castings fragment found near Sully in Glamorgan, very similar to the object listed above. No N.G.R. N.M.W.P.A: 99.34.6.

Lynch-pin terminal made of bronze found at Raglan with a hole pierced through the side for securing to another item. N.G.R: SO 427 071. N.P.T: 88.141.

Bronze lynch pin with decorated lower terminal or foot found at St Arfon's. No N.G.R. N.P.T: 88.104.

Harness mount/strap junction made of cast bronze reportedly recovered from a house in Chepstow whilst the foundations were undergoing construction (Savory 1976: 61). This example is in the form of an S-scroll with knobbed terminals. The knobs are decorated with concentric rings of red and possibly, yellow opaque glass, similar in form to those at Polden Hill (Brailsford 1975) and the Seven Sisters (Spratling and Davies 1976). An electrotype copy is held at The National Museum and Gallery of Wales, Cardiff (Jope 2000: 302 and 312; Fox 1958: 129; Nash-Williams 1932: 393, fig 1). N.G.R: ST 561 939. N.M.W: 35.304. See figure 2.

La Tène, strap union found at Alltwen, Neath, Glamorgan – (Gwilt and Davies forthcoming). This example is best paralleled by material found in the Polden Hills, Santon (Brailsford 1975) and Westhall hoards (Harood 1855). N.G.R: SN 7311 0330. N.M.W: 98.91.H.

Copper alloy terret found at Black Pill Glamorgan. N.G.R: SS 61 90. N.M.W: 98.14.H.

Fragment of a cast alloy oval terret, found near Caerleon, Monmouthshire. This object consists of part of the ring, a moulded collar, part of the integrally cast connecting bar and one plain side knob. The terret tapers from the collar towards it top. The collar is made up of a single moulding that protrudes into the side of the ring. Plain knobbed terrets with domed knobs (group IXA cf. Spratling 1972:

35-37) are a type most commonly found in southern Scotland and the area around Hadrian's Wall, however, a small number are recorded in southern Britain (Spratling 1972: no's 82-3; MacGregor 1976: 69-71 no's 78-109) making the appearance of this example notable. Another example found in this area of this type of terret, but without enamel decoration, has been found at Neath, Glamorgan (MacGregor 1976: 69). Whilst it is not possible to precisely date this example, the style in which it is made provides a diagnostic date range from the middle of the 1st century AD to the 3rd century AD (Macgregor 1976: 46; MacDonald 2001. A.I.W 2001). N.G.R: ST 323 923. N.M.W.P.A: 2001.26.1.

Pottery

Two Iron Age pottery sherds were recovered from Broughton Burrows, Glamorgan. N.G.R: SS 92 71 N.M.W: 78.41.H.6 and 78.41.H.4.

Pottery fragments of Early Iron Age date found at Burrow Wells. No N.G.R. N.M.W: 53.459.11.

Three pieces of pottery including one central body sherd, a section of double beaded rim and a single rim sherd. These were found near Caerwent quarry. N.G.R: ST 47 90. N.P.T: 84.05.5.

Early Iron Age Pottery found near Colcot. No N.G.R. N.M.W: 62.92.1.

Late Iron Age pottery, found at Magor. N.G.R: ST 418 862. N.P.T: 87.461.

Iron Age material recovered by chance behind the inner rampart at Nash Point, Marcross. N.G.R: SS 915 685. The finds consist of a small plain potsherd of soapy, well-smoothed grey ware, limpet shells and beach pebbles. N.G.R: SS 915 684. N.M.W: 59.104.1-3.

Two Iron Age pottery sherds found at Minchin Hole Cave. N.G.R: SS 555 869. N.M.W: 2000.66.H1 + H2.

Iron Age pottery sherd with comb-lined decoration, found near Chapel Tump. N.P.T: 85.218.6.

Iron Age pottery sherd found at Rumney Great Wharf, Cardiff. N.G.R: ST 240 784. N.M.W: 75.20H.

Two pottery sherds, dated to either the Late Iron Age or early Roman were found at Waterstone. No N.G.R. N.M.W: 88.10.H.16 through 88.10.H.18.

Production

Pelter shaped ingot, unknown provenance. Similar to one recovered from the Seven Sisters hoard from Glamorgan (Davies and Spratling 1976). No N.G.R. N.M.W.P.A: 2001.123.46.

Religious

Bronze stylised horse figurine found whilst digging a garden of an old cottage at Pentwyn-mawr near Abercarn. The figuring is made of bronze and represents a horse in a stylised manner somewhat suggestive of continental La Tène traditions (Savory 1952: 72-3). This piece is to be included in a forthcoming paper by A Gwilt (Gwilt pers comm). No N.G.R. N.M.W: 49.4. See figure 3.

Cult Pillar made of sandstone (Savory 1976: 77). This object was found incorporated in a wall at the junction of the western ends of Pen-y-cae and Gwar-y-caeau roads on the outskirts of Port Talbot (Megaw 1964: 94-8). The stone is reminiscent of a group of native stone carvings from Britain and continental Europe dated to the early centuries AD that continue the Celtic veneration of the human head which in artistic form can be dated as far back as the 6th century BC (Megaw 1964: 94-8; Green 2001: 97-106). N.G.R: SS 773 898. N.M.W: 53.262. See figure 4.

Tools

Large axe of either Late Bronze Age or very Early Iron Age date, found at Newton Moor, Penllyn. N.G.R: SS 98 75. N.M.W: 97.31H.

Socketed looped axe of Iron Age date found at Penllyn. No N.G.R.N.M.W: 97.13H. 1.

Iron shaft hole axe, Iron Age or possible Roman date found at Penllyn. No N.G.R. N.M.W: 97.13H.2.

Unknown

Mount for unknown object, possible vessel lid, made of cast bronze, fantastic-grotesque in form, found near Chepstow. No N.G.R. N.P.T: 89.223.

Weapons

Bronze sword-hilt cast onto an iron tang; the pommel is a separate casting and is dated to the Late Iron Age. This example was found in the collection of the former Museum of the Monmouthshire and Caerleon Antiquarian Association (now the Legionary Museum Caerleon), with no recorded provenance (Savory 1976: 61; Boon 1974: 205; Jope 2000 280-1). N.M.W: 31.78. See figure 5.

Worms Head, Rhossili, Glamorgan. N.G.R: SS 386 877.

The following is a collection of material picked up at various times from occupation layers that have been eroded by the sea along the cliff's edge.

A plain disc shaped stone spindle whorl (Savory 1976: 66). N.M.W: 24.117.5

A plain pebble shaped spindle whorl (Savory 1976: 66). N.M.W: 24.117.6.

A stone disc with a projecting ear from which runs a flat-bottomed groove (Savory 1976: 66). N.M.W: 24.117.3.

A fragment from a stone disc that is thought to have originated in Cornwall (Savory 1976: 66). This example has a carefully shaped and smoothed flat-bottomed circular recess on each face. N.M.W: 24.117.4. (Savory 1976: 66).
A stone mould used for the manufacture of objects in an early La Téne style (Savory 1974). N.M.W: 24.117.1. See figure 6.

A deer antler tine, formed by shaving of the beam to form a ledge immediately above the burr. N.M.W: 24.117.2.

The following is a collection of Iron Age material that was recovered from a hearth at the foot of a steep scarp behind Woodfield Terrace, Radyr, Glamorgan. (Savory 1976: 66). N.G.R: ST 134 983.

Early Iron Age pottery. N.M.W: 20.319.1.

Flint flakes, potboilers and fragments of charcoal. N.M.W: 20.319.2. through to N.M.W: 20.319.5.

The following is a variety of material culture that has been recovered from Merthyr Mawr Warren. N.G.R: SS 862 768; the collection and recording of this material has taken place over a number of decades and has been collected from a number of locations at Merthyr Mawr Warren. The following objects were all found at the same location N.G.R: SS 862 768: (Savory 1976: 66).

Four crucible fragments. N.M.W: 01.363.3.

Collection of bronze drops and jets from bronze smelting. N.M.W: 01.363.4.

Miscellaneous small iron objects. N.M.W: 01.363.5.

The following items were found at various locations near the Iron Age site on Merthyr Mawr Warren: (Savory 1976: 67).

Pair of bronze tweezers. N.M.W: 27.380.1.

Bronze bar, looped originally at both ends. The loop is broken, possible chain part. N.M.W: 27.380.2.

Fragments of an iron ring; the end of one of the fragments is thickened with a small knob, possibly part of pennanular brooch. N.M.W: 27.380.3.

Three iron nails. N.M.W: 27.380.4.

Bronze round headed pin, with thin washer attached to it. N.M.W: 27.380.5.

Small fragments of folded bronze plate. N.M.W: 27.380.6.

Fragments of bronze chain. N.M.W: 27.380.7.

Piece of bronze in the shape of a rhomboid. N.M.W: 27.380.8.

Fragments of pottery rim from a handmade vessel. N.M.W: 27.380.9.

Merthyr Mawr Warren

The following two items were picked up during 1938 on or near the Iron Age site (Savory 1976: 67). No N.G.R.

Curved iron knife-blade badly corroded. N.M.W. 42.65.1.

Iron Age pottery including two rim fragments from handmade ovoid jars with beaded rims. N.M.W: 42.65.2.

Merthyr Mawr Warren

Exact location of the next item is not known but presumed to be on or near the Iron Age site (Savory 1976: 67). No N.G.R.

Fragment of pottery containing shell grits. The fragments had a well-smoothed grey surface. N.M.W: 38.656.

Merthyr Mawr Warren

The following material was picked up at various times on or near the site (Savory 1976: 68). No N.G.R.

Bronze needle with lozenge shaped eye. N.M.W: 50.466.21.

Conical shaped button possibly made of shale. N.M.W: 50.466.4.

Fragments of bronze ring or pennanular brooch. N.M.W: 50.466.22.

Bronze pin with plain flattened head. N.M.W: 50.466.23.

Miscellaneous bronze fragments. N.M.W: 50.466.24.

Jets and pearls from bronze founding. N.M.W: 50.466.25.

Fragments of a hearth wall. N.M.W: 50.466.26.

Crucible fragments. N.M.W: 50.466.27.

Pieces of slag waste. N.M.W: 50.466.28.

Section of cylindrical handle of hollowed antler. N.M.W: 50.466.29.

Burnt and fragmented check-piece of a bridle-bit made from antler with a broken perforation at each end. N.M.W: 50.466.30.

Badly corroded La Téne Ic brooch with rounded bow and footplate. N.M.W: 50.466.31

La Téne III, brooch or maybe Romano-British type badly corroded. N.M.W: 50.466.32.

La Téne III, brooch or maybe Romano-British type badly corroded. N.M.W: 50.466.33.

Miscellaneous metal work fragments. N.M.W: 50.466.34.

Net stone sinker, violin shaped. N.M.W: 50.466.35.

Fragment of upper section of beehive quern stone. N.M.W: 50.466.36.

Spheroid bead made of pale green glass. N.M.W: 50.466.37.

Pottery sherd decorated with soft grooves, concentric circles, notched lines and stamped duck-pattern cables, continental tradition. (Savory 1951: 170). N.M.W: 50.466.38.

Undecorated plain grey pottery fragments. N.M.W: 50.466.39.

Merthyr Mawr Warren

Next item found north west of the Iron Age site. No N.G.R.

Two fragments of a bronze ring or pennanular brooch with transverse corrugation of the outer edge. N.M.W: 53.135.5.

Burrows Well and Merthyr Mawr Warren

The following was picked up on between the two sites (Savory 1976: 68). No N.G.R.

Fragments of Iron Age pottery including two fragments from a shouldered jar. N.M.W: 53.459.11.

Merthyr Mawr Warren

The next four items were picked up at various times on of near the Iron Age site. No N.G.R.

Flint scrapper. N.M.W.456.9.

Iron Age pottery sherds. N.M.W: 465.8.

Iron Age pottery sherd. N.M.W: 88.205.H.1-2.

Undated copper alloy metalworking waste. N.M.W: 1898.273.22.

Discussion

The above list gives the reader an insight into the types of artefacts that have been categorised as chance finds. This type of list, whilst limited in what information it can offer, provides locations and in some cases, contexts and dates for the finds. In addition, the items discussed above can add to existing typologies and will assist in the creation of new ones. The undertaking of an exercise such as this illustrates the potential for research in many areas. A good example is the large quantity of material culture recovered from Merthyr Mawr Warren. Most of the artefacts recovered are from various locations across the Warren, however, little exploratory work has been done on any of the objects recovered with the exception of the analysis conducted upon ceramic residues and droplets of bronze by Peter Northover (Gwilt 2002). Aside from a small exploratory excavation conducted here in 1927 by Cyril Fox (to be discussed in a later chapter), there has not been a modern day archaeological excavation at this site. Merthyr Mawr Warren and its accumulated assemblage show excellent potential for further research.

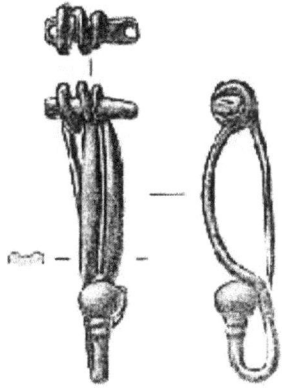

Figure 1. Brooch from Newton Moor.

Figure 2. Harness mount or strap junction from Chepstow

Figure 3. Bronze horse figurine from Abercarn

Figure 4. Cult pillar Port Talbot

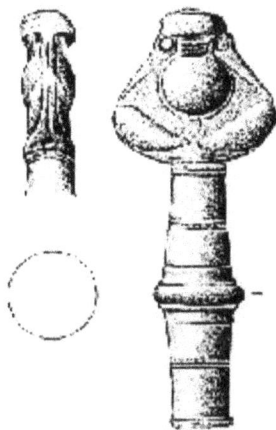

Figure 5. Bronze sword hilt from Caerleon

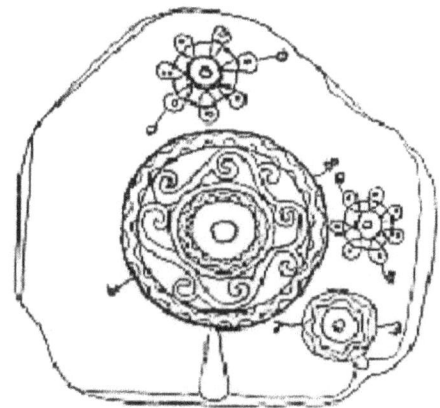

Figure 6. Stone mould from Worms Head

Chapter 4

Hoards: Contexts and Contents

Introduction

Hoards may be defined as an assemblage of objects found together under circumstances that suggest either a single, or in some cases, repeated acts of deposition over a long period of time (Davies 2000: 179). Hoards may have been hidden with the intention of later retrieval or as an act of abandonment, sacrifice or propitiation. The motivation for the deposition of objects can often be ascertained from the character and composition of the hoard and the location from which they are recovered. The locations and contexts of the hoards from south-east Wales vary and the dates applied to each are mainly defined according to the stylistic content rather than through independent dating evidence. In Wales four Iron Age hoards have been recovered from the following sites: Llyn Fawr (LBA/EIA transition), Cardiff (LBA/EIA transition), Seven Sisters (LIA), and Lesser Garth / Pentyrch (LIA); these will form the basis of the following chapter.

Structure of chapter

As the purpose of this investigation is to illustrate the types of material culture that are available within the study area. This chapter will include a brief description of the discovery of each hoard and list the contents for each in an index that is accompanied by images of the objects.

Structure of tables included in text

Included with each hoard is a table that illustrates the amounts of objects in each assemblage; the structure of the tables is described in chapter 1, page 2.

The Llyn Fawr Hoard

The original hoard material at Llyn Fawr was discovered between 1911 and 1913; the first twenty-one items were recovered when the lake near Hirwaun, in Glamorgan was being drained in the course of its conversion into a reservoir. The artifacts were presented to the National Museums and Galleries of Wales by the Rhondda Urban District Council (Crawford and Wheeler 1921; Savory 1976: 46). In 1936, Mr. George Stow, who had been the managing director of the company at the time of the reservoir's construction, sent a letter and another two items; a bronze cauldron and the fragmentary remains of an iron sword to the National Museum and Gallery of Wales, Cardiff (Fox 1939: 369-71). In 1985, Mrs. Anne Butler, the granddaughter of George Stow, brought another two items to the attention of the archaeological world when she confessed to having in her possession two socketed axes that were part of the original hoard recovered from Llyn Fawr. She made these items available to the National Museum and Gallery of Wales, Cardiff, where copies were made, leaving the originals in the possession of Mrs. Butler (Green 1985: 288-9).

Structure of index

The items listed below include a description of each object; the information for which was taken from Savory (1976: 53-4), and accompanying each entry is the National Museum and Gallery of Wales, Cardiff's accession number plus a figure number for images.

Index to Llyn Fawr pieces

1. Bronze looped socketed axe with three slightly divergent ribs on each side and slight moulding around the socket at the top of the loop. This axe has a prominent mouth moulding. N.M.W: 12.11.1. See figure 7.

2. Bronze looped socketed axe with slightly diverging ribs with terminal pellets on each face. The angles have been cast to form ribs with terminal pellets at the same level as the others. N.M.W: 12.11.2. See figure 8.

3. Bronze looped socketed axe; this may have been made from the same mould as object number 2. N.M.W: 12.11.3. See figure 9.

4. Bronze socketed axe with broken loop and large convex mouth moulding, faint moulding on a level with the top of the loop, three divergent ribs with terminal pellets and corresponding pellets at angles. N.M.W: 12.11.4. See figure 10.

5. Bronze looped socketed axe with plain, narrow, undecorated, sub-triangular socket. N.M.W: 12.11.5. See figure 11.

6. Bronze socketed sickle, with socket (two pairs of empty rivet holes) set at right angles to the blade which curves and has a single midrib. N.M.W: 12.11.6. See figure 12.

7. Bronze socketed sickle, with socket (two pairs of empty rivet holes) set at right angles to the blade, which curves and has a single midrib. N.M.W: 12.11.7. See figure 13.

8. Iron socketed sickle with oval section socket in which there is a pair of rivet holes; one with a part of a bronze pin, set at right angles to the curving blade, which has a heavy central midrib. Around the mouth of the socket is a grooved iron ring added for strengthening. This has been welded and is held in place by the turned back edge of the socket. N.M.W: 12.11.8. See figure 14.

9. Bronze socketed gouge with simple mouth moulding. N.M.W: 12.11.9. See figure 15.

10. Bronze socketed gouge with deep collar at mouth. N.M.W: 12.11.10. See figure 16.

11. Bronze socketed gouge with simple mouth moulding. N.M.W:12.11.11. See figure 17.

12. Bronze razor with double looped handle and triangular opening in blade. Razors of similar type from Ham Hill (Gray 1923) and Leckwith, Glamorgan (Piggott 1946). N.M.W: 12.11.12. See figure 18.

13. Fragment of socketed axe similar in form to object numbers 1 to 4, only a portion of the socket remains. N.M.W: 12.11.13.

14. Bronze harness fitting in the form of a domed bronze disc of thin sheet metal. It has a flat turned up rim and a single half round moulding at the edge. At the center of the disc is a small circular plate with rectangular loop at the back for attachment to another object. N.M.W: 12.11.14. See figure 19.

15. Bronze harness fitting similar to object number 14 but has a different rim and lacks the moulding at the edge but has a double convex moulding and central groove along the outer surface. N.M.W: 12.11.15. See figure 20.

16. Bronze harness fitting similar to object number 15 but the central plate is concave and the oval loop at the back is held in place by a rivet. N.M.W: 12.11.16. See figure 21.

17. Winged bronze harness fitting (cheek-piece) with terminal discs displaying concentric circles on the wings. The wings are hollow and open at the top. Along the edge of the opening are two holes on either side. The face is well finished and has raised edges and a curved rib runs across it to link up the disc at each

end. The other face is less well finished and has no raised edges. N.M.W: 12.11.17. See figure 22.

18. Fragment of a bronze harness fitting, similar to object number 17 and appears to be from the same mould. N.M.W: 12.11.18.

19. Bronze harness fitting consisting of a rectangular plate divided vertically into three parts by raised narrow ridges. The middle panel is pierced by six equally spaced rectangular openings. Attached to the lower edge of the plate are five discs with hollowed, moulded, concentric circles fitted around a central boss. There are evenly spaced loops near the top edge of the plate on the back. N.M.W: 12.11.19. See figure 23.

20. Bronze belt hook, hollow casting, closed at one end to the middle and cast in one piece. N.M.W: 12.11.20. See figure 24.

21. Iron socketed spearhead of riveted type. The socket is split and damaged at the mouth. N.M.W: 12.11.21. See figure 25.

22. Bronze cauldron built up of five tiers of metal, of which one circular sheet forms the base, three sheets form the sides, and the fifth sheet forms the shoulder, everted flange and rolled rim. These parts are riveted together with either round or conical headed rivets. As there are pieces of metal missing, it is impossible to tell how many rivets were used in each tier; the fifth tier contains at least two. The beaded rim is bent around a core of heavier tubular strip. The grooved ring handles are held to the cauldron by staples cast in one to the flanges. The flange has been strengthened by two bronze strips riveted to the shoulder, which pass through slots into the flanges. N.M.W: 13.112. See figure 26.

23. Bronze cauldron built of five tiers of sheet metal riveted together with conical headed rivets. The top tier forms the shoulder, everted flange and rolled rim. The angle formed by the shoulder and flange is reinforced with a tube of heavier metal over which the plate has been bent. The grooved ring handles are held to the cauldron by staples, cast directly on to the flange. The lip is well worn. N.M.W: 36.624. See figure 27.

24. Fragmented iron sword of continental Halstatt C type, comprised of the upper part of a moulded blade and part of the handle plate that was made of bone. N.M.W: 36.624.2. See figure 28.

Discussion

The Llyn Fawr hoard has been assigned a Late Bronze Age/Early Iron Age date and gives its name to the period because of the presence of an iron Halstatt 'C' sword which represents one of the first identifiable appearances of iron recorded from Britain (Davies 2000: 183; Northover 1988:

75-85; O'Connor 1980). The inclusion of two bronze cauldrons which are of B1 type and of Irish manufacture are believed to have been several generations old when deposited in the lake; both have been accorded a date of c. 800 BC (Jope 2000: 225-6; Savory 1975; 1976). Other items found in this hoard that are chronologically diagnostic are an iron socketed sickle, an iron spear head and bronze axes, one of which has been submitted for analysis at the 'Oxford Radiocarbon Accelerator Programme'. The single axe was submitted and tests carried out on material recovered from the haft gave a date that falls at 2545 ± 55 BP, calibrating to 830-510 BC (Needham et al 1997: 98-9).

The early date and the inclusion of both iron and bronze objects in the Llyn Fawr hoard is indicative of the social changes that were taking place at the time of deposition. The iron Halstatt 'C' sword and the bronze phalerae or cheek pieces have characteristics comparable examples found in Halstatt 'C' contexts in both France and Belgium and are so well made that it has been suggested that they were imported into Britain from continental Europe (Jope 2000: 226). However, there are iron objects in the hoard representing early attempts at iron working in Britain. These objects include a spear and a socketed sickle that were made in a technique better suited to bronze casting, suggesting that the metal smiths who made these items had a limited knowledge of working with iron (Avery 1993: 101). Examples of early iron objects found in other areas of Britain are present in Bronze Age hoards at Sompting in Sussex (Curwen 1948) and from Colchester in Essex (Hawkes and Smith 1957).

Figures 7, 8, 9, 10 and 11. Axes   **Figures 12, 13 and 14**. Sickles

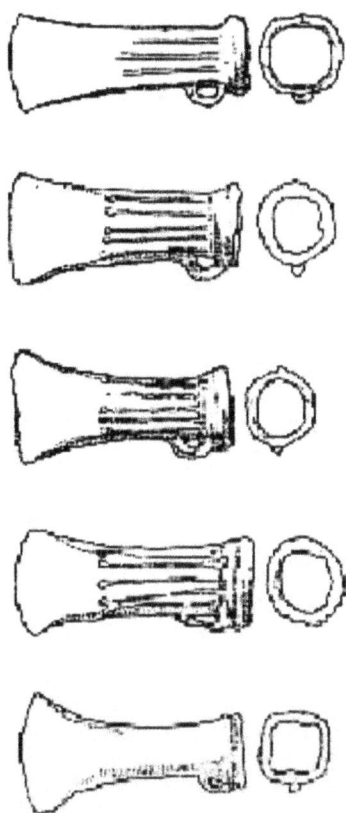 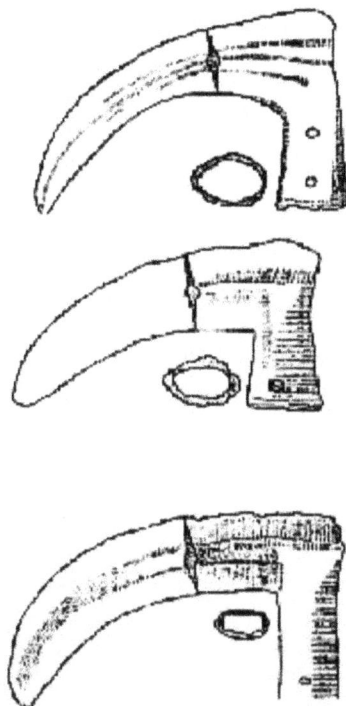

Figure 15

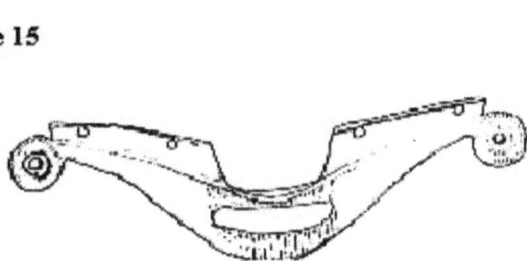 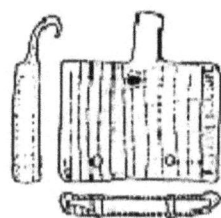 

17

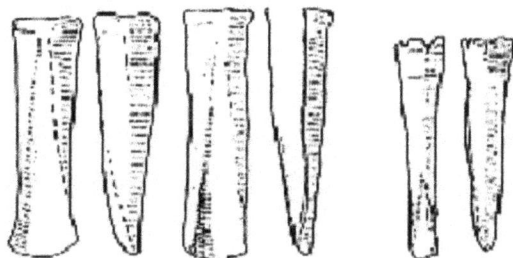 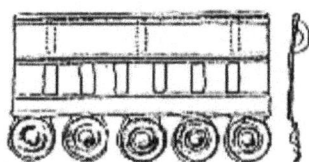 

Figure 25. Iron spearhead

Figure 19. Bronze harness disc from Llyn Fawr

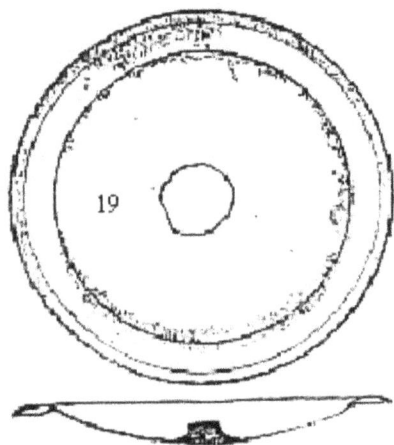

Figure 28. Iron sword from Llyn Fawr

Figure 20. Bronze harness disc from Llyn Fawr

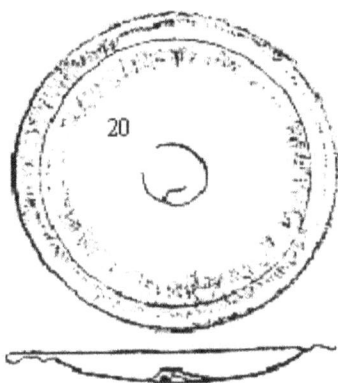

Figure 21. Bronze harness disc from Llyn Fawr

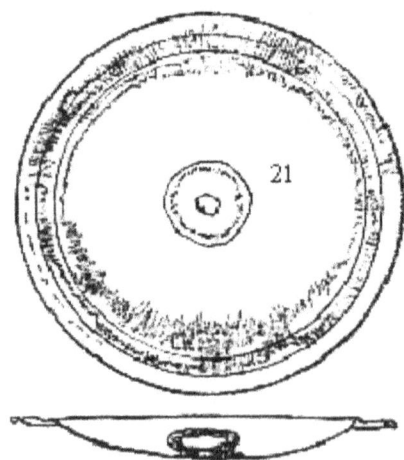

Figure 26. Cauldron from Llyn Fawr

Figure 2
Cauldron from Llyn Fa

17

The Cardiff Hoard

The Cardiff hoard was discovered in 1928 at Leckwith in a shallow bed of river-sand on the flood plains of the Rivers Taff and Ely near Cardiff in Glamorgan. The objects were sold to an antiques dealer from whom Mr. F. E. Andrews bought them before presenting them to the National Museum and Gallery of Wales, Cardiff. (Nash-Williams 1933).

Structure of index

To follow is a description of each object; the information for each was taken from either Savory (1976: 53) or from Nash-Williams (1933: 299) and accompanying each entry will be the National Museum and Gallery of Wales, Cardiff accession number plus a figure number for images.

Index to the Cardiff Hoard

1. Socketed axe, looped with three diverging ribs on each face with terminal bosses attached near the moulded mouth of the socket to a slight moulding on a level with the base of the loop. N.M.W: 30.130.1. See figure 29.

2. Socketed axe, square socketed variety consisting of part of mouth of socket with loop, similar to object number 1 in this group. N.M.W: 30.130.2. See figure 30.

3. Socketed chisel, socket damaged with a wide expanded blade. N.M.W: 30.130.3. See figure 31.

4. Socketed chisel, undamaged, with wide expanded blade, similar in form to object 3 with a pair of rivet holes inside the socket near the mouth. N.M.W: 30.130.4. . See figure 32.

5. Socketed chisel similar to objects number 4, but the edge is turned back at the ends and there is a narrow grooved collar around the mouth of the socket. N.M.W: 30.130.5. See figure 33.

6. Socketed chisel similar to objects 4 and 5 but with small blade and a simple narrow collar around the mouth of the socket. N.M.W: 30.130.6. See figure 3.

7. Square-socketed sickle with the central rib of the blade stopping short at the sockets; a feature that indicates that this implement is earlier typologically than those in which the rib is carried across the socket. N.M.W: 30.130.7. See figure 35.

8. Sickle blade fragment of socketed type with three narrow ribs that converge towards the point on each face. The fragment is bent and twisted N.M.W: 30.130.8. . See figure 36

9. Razor of double-edged circular type from which the tang is missing. It has a triangular opening in the centre of the blade and a narrow slit on top dividing the edge into two parts. N.M.W: 30.130.9. See figure 37.

10. Razor of triangular type with single edge, a small looped handle and triangular opening in the blade. N.M.W: 30.130.10. See figure 38.

11. Cap of chariot pole. This is a cylindrical casting and is damaged with two large roughly circular openings; one is broken. N.M.W: 30.130.11. See figure 39.

Discussion

The Cardiff hoard consists of eleven pieces of bronze metal work which have been assigned a similar date range as the Llyn Fawr hoard because of the inclusion of Halstatt derivatives. Some of the tools are distinctive and are chronologically diagnostic including two large ribbed and pellet axes (one fragmentary), which are a variation of the square-socketed variety (Northover 1988: 80) as is the sickle. The central rib of the sickle blade stops short at the socket; a feature that places the sickle chronologically earlier than examples where the rib is carried across the socket as in the sickles at Llyn Fawr. There are also two derivatives of Halstatt type razors: one is circular with a triangular central opening and a stump of a tang handle remains and the other is similar in form to one found in the Llyn Fawr hoard. The second example has a crescentric blade with a triangular opening and a looped handle and both examples are very rare in Britain. The chisels are of a general form with triangular blades and a conical socket separated by a pronounced collar moulding. The remaining piece of this hoard is made of cast metal, cylindrical in shape and is believed to be a chariot pole fitting. A similar example can be found in the Llyn Cerrig Bach hoard (Fox 1946; Savory 1976: 83, fig 4; Nash-Williams 1933).

Figure 31. Chisel from Cardiff

Figure 29. Axe from Cardiff

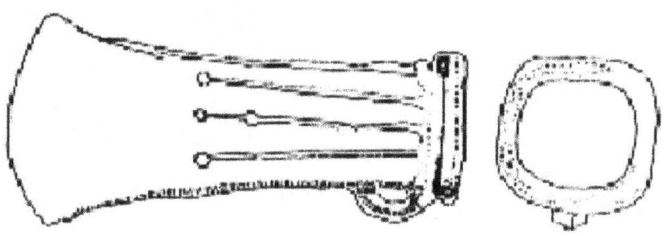

Figure 32. Chisel from Cardiff

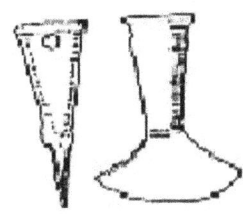

Figure 30. Axe from Cardiff

Figure 33. Chisel from Cardiff

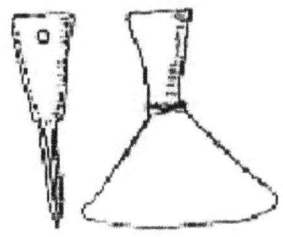

Figure 35. Sickle from Cardiff

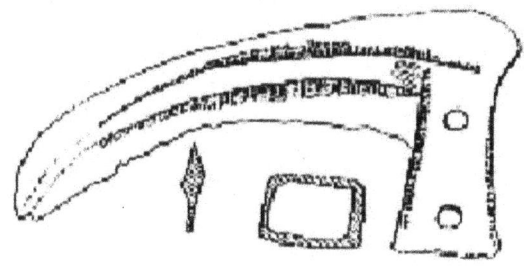

Figure 34. Chisel from Cardiff

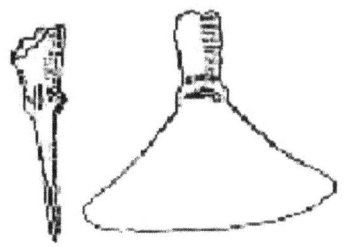

Figure 36. Sickle from Cardiff

Figure 39. Chariot cap from Cardiff

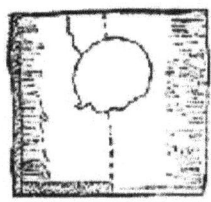

Figures 37 and 38. Triangular and circular razors from Cardiff

19

The Seven Sisters Hoard

The Seven Sisters hoard of bronzes (Allen 1905; Davies & Spratling 1976) was discovered in a streambed near Neath in Glamorgan after a severe storm had caused major floods in 1875. Whilst every endeavor has been made to clarify the exact location of the find spot of the hoard, the exact location has not been agreed. The items in this hoard can be grouped into three categories: those that are Roman in character, those that are indigenous in character, and those that can be placed in either group (Davies and Spratling 1976). All the objects are constructed of bronze.

Structure of index

To follow is a description of each object; the information for each was taken from Savory (1976: 63), Davies and Spratling (1976: 125-135) and the National Museum and Gallery of Wales, Cardiff accompanying each entry will be accession number, and a figure number for images, where applicable.

Index to the Seven Sisters Hoard

1. Terminal rings; one of two bronze rings for a three-link bridle-bit with rings and side-links cast in a one-piece and central ornament. This piece also has sunken panels that retain some traces of red opaque glass/enamel. D & S: 16. N.M.W: 04.125. See figure 40.

2. Terminal rings; one of two bronze rings for a three-link bridle-bit with rings and side-links cast in a one piece and central ornament. D & S: 16. N.M.W: 04.126. See figure 41.

3. Terrets of cast bronze with insets on the three knobs for *champlevé* enamel. Enough of the enamel has survived to reconstruct the original colors used; the pointed oval cells were inlaid with white enamel, the triangular ones with red. This piece shows signs of wear around the top of each stop. D & S: 19, N.M.W: 04.127. See figure 42.

4. Terret of cast bronze identical to object number 3 except that there is no sign of wear on the stops indicating that this piece may have been unused. The piece cannot have come from the same mould because the sizes are different. D & S: 20. N.M.W: 04.128. See figure 43.

5. Terret of cast bronze, incomplete with the larger part of the ring missing. On one side of the scalloped edge of the flange above the attachment loop is damaged. The presence of a flash line along the underside of the flange to one side is indicative of casting in a one-piece mould. Parallels at Corbridge (Bishop and Dore 1988) and Newstead (Curle 1911). D & S: 9. N.M.W: 04.129.

6. Strap union made of cast bronze, strap ring and strap end, each embellished on the obverse with insets, some of which are now empty but others are filled with black alloy. There are no close parallels to this particular piece but comparisons have been made with pieces from Brecon Gaer (Casey 1971), Colchester (Hawkes and Hull 1947) and Hod Hill (Richmond 1968). D & S: 1. N.M.W: 04.130. See figure 45.

7. Strap union made of cast bronze that are plain on the back where there are two projecting loops. The obverse is covered with insets for *champlevé* enamel of red and bluish white. D & S: 17. N.M.W: 04.131. See figure 44.

8. Buckle made of cast bronze. When examined in 1963, the hinge pinholes were filled with iron that has since disappeared. Paralleled to buckles found at Richborough (Bushe-Fox 1949) and Wroxeter (White and Barker 1998). D & S: 10. N.M.W: 04.132.

9. Strap slide mount made of cast bronze with a pair of domed ornamental rivets of an original set of four attached to the main panel. One of the terminal loops is broken and incomplete. The concave sides of the principle loop appear to be an original feature of the design and not the result of wear. Unparalleled. D & S: 5. N.M.W:04.133. See figure 46.

10. Pendant made of bronze it has silver or tin-leaf overlay on one side and is plain on the other. This piece is decorated with a chased engraved foliate pattern originally filled with inlay. Parallels at Fremington Hagg (Webster 1958; MacGregor 1976) and Wroxeter (White and Barker 1998). D & S: 3. N.M.W: 04.134. See figure 48.

11. Triangular strap union made of cast bronze mount. This piece is complete except for two broken coils at the corners with two damaged bronze strap-ends of an original set of three. No known parallels but compares to a strap end from Wroxeter (White and Barker 1998). D & S: 4. N.M.W: 04.135. See figure 49.

12. Pendant-hook made of cast bronze in two pieces with red enamel and inset in two terminals in *champlevé* technique. All the insets except the triangular one on the side of the terminal are bordered by fine chased or engraved lines. D & S: 14. N.M.W: 04.136.

13. Pendant-hook incomplete. Identical to object number 18 and paralleled to a pair of objects from Polden Hill (Brailsford 1975), however, their identification as trace-hooks has not been substantiated (Fox 1958: 125). D & S: 14. N.M.W: 04.137.

14. Tankard handle made of cast bronze in perfect condition except for some damage to one of the terminals. The profile of the handle indicates that it was designed for attachment to a concave walled vessel. D & S: 21. N.M.W: 04.138. See figure 50.

15. Tankard handle made of cast bronze with badly damaged terminals. The lesser-damaged terminal has a circular nail hole. The profile of the handle indicates that it was designed for attachment to a concave walled vessel. D & S: 22. N.M.W: 04.139. See figure 51.

16. Tankard handle made of cast bronze in two pieces with chased or engraved linear ornament and tiny annular faces impressed with a fine ring-punch. There are circular nail holes in each terminal. The profile of the handle indicates that it was designed for attachment to a concave walled vessel. D & S: 23. N.M.W: 04.140. See figure 52.

17. Tankard handle made of cast bronze, incomplete with one terminal missing. On the grip is what remains of three cross-scored domes; it is possible that the cross-scoring was intended for enamel inlay as seen on the horned helmet that was found near Waterloo Bridge in 1868 (Franks 1854; Fox 1958: 49-50; Megaw 1970; Jope 2000: 255), although no trace of enamel remains on this handle. Parallels at Hod Hill (Richmond 1968). D & S: 24. N.M.W: 04.141. See figure 53.

18. Tankard handle made of wrought bronze with nail holes to one side of the central axis. Paralleled to handles from Newstead (Curle 1911). D & S: 25. N.M.W: 04.142. See figure 54.

19. Disc of sheet bronze that appears to have been broken from a larger object, with a domed stud attached in the center. Considered to be part of a phalera and is paralleled to pieces from Fremington Hagg (Webster 1958; MacGregor 1976). D & S: 2. N.M.W: 04.143. See figure 47.

20. Ring made of cast bronze incomplete and badly corroded. D & S: 13. N.M.W: 04.144.

21. Helmet crest knob made of bronze. The basal flange has a damaged edge and three regularly spaced rivet holes. There is a generic resemblance to crest-knobs on a variety of helmets; see Robinson 1975. D & S: 12. N.M.W: 04.145.

22. Bell; incomplete cast bronze with ragged lower edge. Neither the clapper nor stumps for its attachment survives within the rounded square sounding box. Paralleled to a bell from Richmond. D & S: 7. N.M.W: 04.146.

23. Bell; incomplete cast bronze with ragged lower edge. The suspension loop has been broken off. The two stumps of the clapper attachment survive inside the sounding box. Paralleled with a bell from Hod Hill (Richmond 1968). D & S: 8. N.M.W: 04.147.

24. Circular fragment in two pieces of a hollow object made of cast bronzes and includes insets that would have originally held inlay. There is a circular rivet or nail hole just below a decorated frieze. No parallels but similar to object number 7. D & S: 6. N.M.W: 04.148.

25. Balance weight made of cast bronze with a Roman numeral 'I' chased into one face. The weight of the piece is 309.5 grammes and is recognized as a standard 'Celtic pound' employed in north-western and central Europe in the Late Iron Age and Roman period (Spratling in Rowley & Cunliffe 1973;). D & S: 11. N. M.W: 04.149.

26. Ingot made of bronze and is badly corroded. This ingot weighs 204.2 grammes and is close to two thirds of the standard 'Celtic pound' (see above) and is indicative of the careful measuring of metal weights before melting and pouring. D & S 26. N.M.W: 04.150.

27. Ingot made of bronze weighing 147.0 grammes. This piece is badly corroded and is two pieces. D & S: 27. N.M.W: 04.151.

28. Casting jet, bronze jet from the spruce cup of a mould. A flash line indicates the mould was composite. D & S: 29. N.M.W: 04.152.

29. Casting jet, bronze jet from the spruce cup of a mould. D & S: 30. N.M.W: 04.153.

30. Billet; severely corroded damaged piece of wrought metal with elongated facets from a pane-hammer just detectable on the face. The shape of this piece suggests the object was in the early stages of manufacture rather than an off cut of metal. D & S: 32. N.M.W: 04.154.

31. Billet cast bronze in two fragments. A small group of elongated facets from a pane-hammer are visible in the center of the draw face of the larger fragment. D & S: 31. N.M.W: 04.155.

32. Lump of sheet metal folded in two and hammered into a tight lump. D & S: 33. N.M.W: 04.156.

33. Lump of sheet metal folded in two and hammered into a tight lump. D & S: 34. N.M.W: 04.156.

34. Lump of sheet metal folded in two and hammered into a tight lump. Objects numbered 33, 34 and 35 were probably prepared for the melting pot. D & S: 35. N.M.W: 04.156.

35. Lump of casting bronze. D & S: 28. N.M.W: 04.157.

36. Strap union almost identical to object number 7 (above) except for the weight and small differences in size, indicating that they were made in different moulds. Paralleled to similar type at Chepstow, Gwent (Nash-Williams 1932; Grimes 1939; Taylor and Brailsford 1985). British Museum.

Discussion

The Seven Sisters hoard has been assigned a late 1st century AD date, achieved through the diagnostic analogy of the stylistic components of the enamel inlays on the decorated metal work, plus the inclusion of Roman military equipment (Davies and Spratling 1976). There are five tankard handles present and their profiles show that three of the handles were made for attachment to tankards that had concave sides. The handles have proved difficult to date as no stylistic parallels can be found, although various elements of their stylistic attributes can be found on tankard handles at Hod Hill in Dorset (Richmond 1968) Waddon in Stoke Abbott (Corcoran 1952) and Newstead, Roxburghshire (Curle 1933)

Davies suggests (2000a: 11) that the hoard belonged to an indigenous metal worker and that the incorporation of both Roman cavalry equipment and indigenous objects may be the result of successful skirmishes against Roman forces during the Roman incursion into Wales. It is highly unlikely that the Roman army would have given or traded such objects to their enemy, for when the Romans finished with this type of material, it was usually returned to a *fabrica* for recycling (www.roman-britain.org/glossary_m.htm). Another suggestion is that the objects came into indigenous hands as part of a diplomatic gift, but whether the Romans or British bestowed the gifts remains a matter of conjecture (Davies and Spratling 1976: 140).

The items in the Seven Sisters hoard can be divided into three groups, and in contrast to Davies and Spratlings (1976) divisions of Roman, native British or Roman-British, a division of horse equipment and production pieces would appear more workable. All the pieces included in this hoard can be described as fragmentary. A close examination of the hoard as a whole and not just of the metal objects, illustrates the diverse nature of the collection. A large percentage of the items could have been used for the repair or manufacture of other objects and were probably the property of an individual who collected fragments for this purpose.

Figure 41. Bridle bit ring

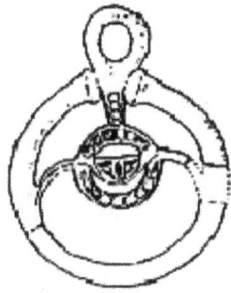

Figure 42. Terret

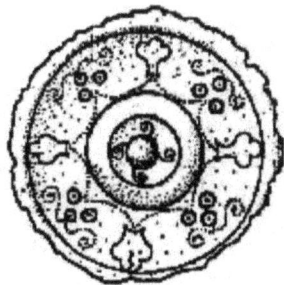

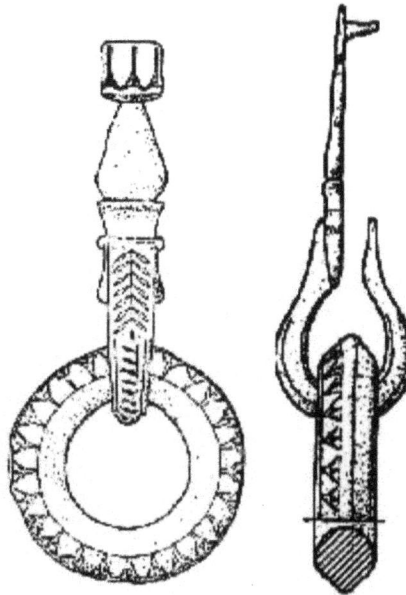

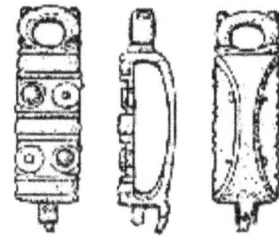

Figure 48. Bronze pendent

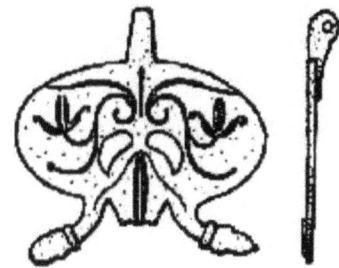

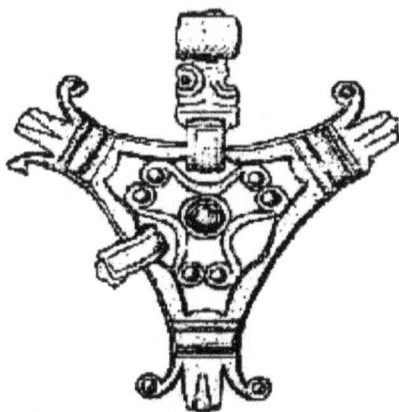

Figure 53. Tankard handle

Figure 51. Tankard handle

Figure 54. Tankard handle

Figure 52. Tankard handle

23

The Lesser Garth - Pentyrch Hoard

The final group in this category was discovered in a quarry in Pentyrch, Glamorgan in 1965. Lesser Garth is renown for the cave systems that have yielded artefacts from the Bronze Age to the Early Medieval periods (Hussey 1964-66) and this hoard was recovered during the removal of topsoil in a quarry, approximately 200 yards from one of the caves (Manning 1972).

Structure of index

To follow is a description of each object, the information for which was taken from Savory (1976: 63-4; Savory 1966) and accompanying each entry will be the National Museum and Gallery of Wales, Cardiff accession number and a figure number for images.

Index to the Pentyrch Hoard

1. Terret ring made of cast bronze inlayed with red enamel. This terret ring is one of the finest examples of its kind in Britain. N.M.W: 65.82.1. See figure 55.

2. Bridle-bit made of iron, fragmentary with a single curving bar, sub-rectangular in section, curled round at the complete end to hold a surviving side ring. This is probably a bridle-bit for a cart-horse (Savory 1966: 33). An example of this type is present in the Llyn Cerrig Bach hoard (Fox 1946; MacDonald 2000). N.M.W: 65.82.1. See figure 56.

3. Cauldron ring and staple, made of iron and is massive in stature with a staple attached. It is thought to be for the suspension of a cauldron-type known from the La Tène site (Vouga 1923: 81, plate. XXVII.2). This type of cauldron has a sheet bronze body riveted to its upper edge and a broad strip of iron which forms the rim with two tubular staples riveted to it. A parallel for this object can be found at Letchworth, Hertfordshire. (Smith 1913-14; Savory 1966: 38). N.M.W: 65.82.3. See figure 57.

4. Lynch-pin with a heavy iron bar that is incomplete at the lower end. It has had one end beaten out into a broad semi-circular head and is probably a lynch-pin for a cart. A similar type has been recorded in the Romano-British Hoard from Eckford, Roxburghshire (Piggott 1952; MacGregor 1976; Savory 1966: 33). N.M.W: 65.82.4. See figure 58.

5. Cauldron Hanger made of iron. The ring is stout and is attached to the broadened looped end of a bar. Thought to be part of a cauldron chain paralleled to examples from Standfordbury, Bedfordshire (Smith 1909; Fox 1923) this type has looped rods incorporated with chain-

links. The rods are often twisted near the centre (Savory 1966: 38). N.M.W: 65.82.5. See figure 59.

6. Knife made of iron and is single edged, the blade is broken off and the tang is coiled at the end (Savory 1796: 64). The coiling of the end of the tang simulates the ring found in some of the continental late La Tène knife handles; this type of construction persists into the Roman period (Savory 1966: 35). N.M.W: 65.82.6. See figure 60.

7. Chisel made of iron. It is very large with a cylindrical section. The tip is damaged and hammering has spread the head of the chisel. A number of parallels can be found at La Tène (Vouga 1926: 12-17), Hod Hill (Richmond 1968) Vol 1, 14 fig 13) and Rotherley in Wiltshire (Pitt-Rivers 1888). The examples cited are much smaller than the Pentyrch example (Savory 1966: 35). N.M.W: 65.82.7. See figure 61.

8. Iron billet; this is a tapering iron bar that appears to be a billet of raw material, partially shaped to reform into another object. It is difficult to find a parallel for this piece in Britain (Savory 1966: 36). N.M.W: 65.82.8. See figure 62.

9. Latch-lifter; this is a section of curving iron bar, which is broken off at each end. The bar is made from a rectangular section and bends near the middle. Latch-lifters were normally made from a rectangular section bar in the early Iron Age as found at Glastonbury (Bullied and Gray 1911) and Hunsbury Camp, Northamptonshire (Fell 1936). Latch-lifters continued to be used into the Roman period and are found at Park Street, St Alban's Villa and Verulamium (Wheeler 1936), however, these later examples tend to have a circular section bar. N.M.W: 65.82.9. See figure 63.

10. Knife. Coiled terminal of the tang of a single bladed knife similar to object number 6. This example is badly corroded (Savory 1976: 64). N.M.W: 65.82.10. See figure 64.

11. Iron ring. Corroded remains of iron ring with four attached double links that could be part of a suspension chain from a cauldron (Savory 1976: 66). N.M.W: 65.82.11. See figure 65.

Discussion

The Lesser Garth hoard consists mainly of iron objects and a bronze terret that through chronological diagnosis has produced a date of the mid 1st century AD (Savory 1966). Manning argues, however, that it could be of a later date as it is similar in typology to those hoards found at Waltham Abbey, Essex and Santon, Downham, Norfolk (Smith 1908-9; Manning 1972: 231-2). Whilst a Late Iron Age date may be acceptable for this collection, caution is needed here. Single coloured red enamels were being exploited from c.100 BC through to the 1st century AD suggesting that the hoard could be dated to anytime between the mentioned dates and thus a wider date bracket may apply. However, other diagnostic pieces in the collection include a variety of iron objects that have parallels at Santon, Downham, Norfolk (Smith 1908-9) Polden Hill; Somerset (Brailsford 1975) as well as Seven Sisters, Glamorgan (Davies and Spratling 1976). These sites have a date of the mid 1st century AD so it is plausible that this date range could be applied to the Lesser Garth hoard.

Table 5. Llyn Fawr and Cardiff hoards

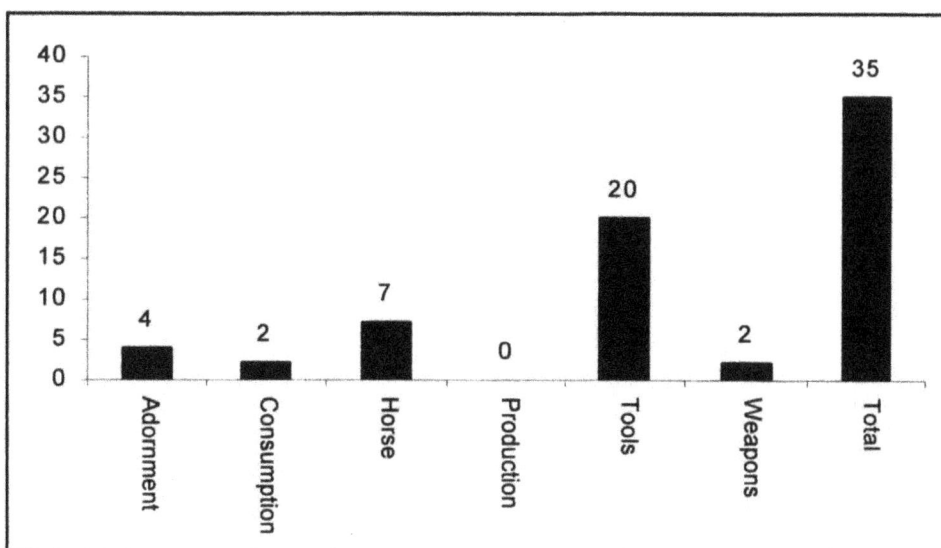

Table 6. Seven Sisters and Lesser Garth/Pentyrch hoards

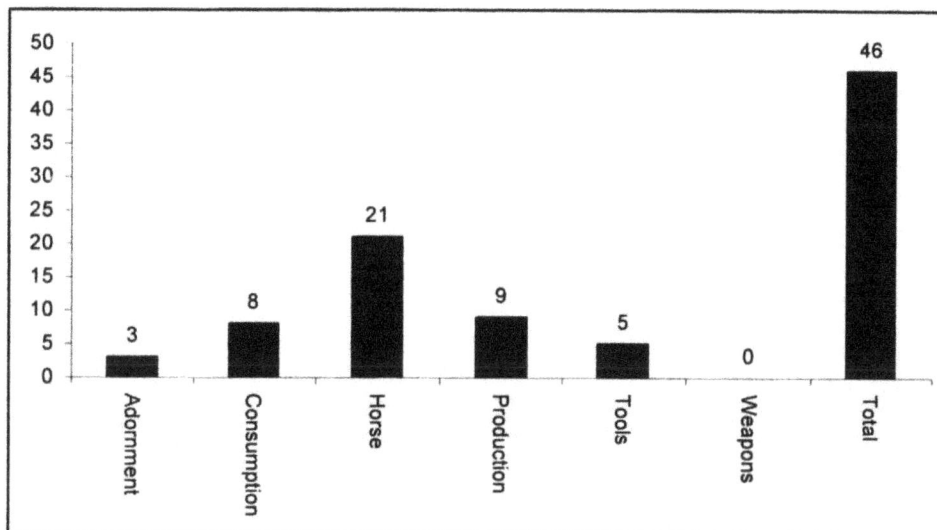

Figure 55. Iron bridle bit

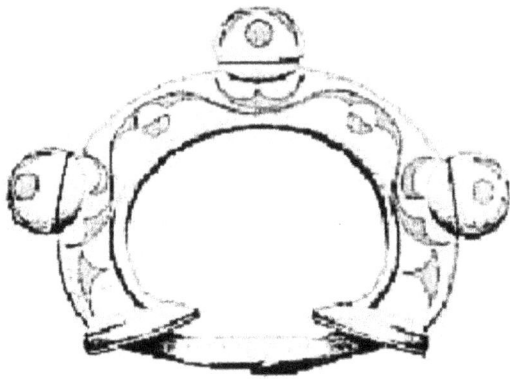

Figure 57. Cauldron hanger and staple

Figure 56. Chisel

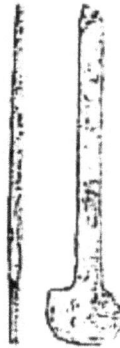

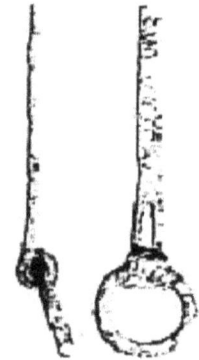

Figure 58. Bridle bit

Figure 61. Iron chisel

Figure 60. Cauldron ring and staple

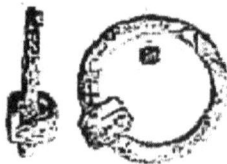

Figure 62. Iron knife

Figure 63. Iron billet

Figure 64. Iron knife

Figure 66. Cauldron chain

Figure 65. Latch lifter

Conclusion

Hoards have been recovered from a variety of contexts such as bogs, marshes, springs, wells, and rivers as well as from many dry locations such as Appleford in Berkshire (Brown 1971), Pentyrch in Glamorgan (Savory 1966) and Hamden Hill in Somerset (Hoare 1825). Hoards of metal work dating to the Early Iron Age are, for the most part, a rare occurrence (Manning 1988: 239). The earliest hoards such as those from Llyn Fawr (Crawford And Wheeler 1921) and Cardiff (Nash-Williams 1933) can be placed in the transitional phase of the Late Bronze Age/Early Iron Age period. It is not until the Late Iron Age that all kinds of metal objects were being deposited in bogs like Blackburn Mill, Berwickshire (Piggott 1953) and Carlingwark Loch, Kirkcudbrights (Curle 1932) and also in places like the rivers Thames and Witham (Stead 1985, Field 1983: 194; Green 1986). It appears that towards the end of the Iron Age, concurrently with the incursion of the Roman Empire, hoarding once again become part of the social/ritual activity of the people of this period. Whether or not this was a direct result of the possible tensions arising at this time between the indigenous population and the Romans is difficult to say but an increase in depositional hoarding is clearly evident.

The examination of the stylistic trends of these objects and any identification of any parallels available are important when looking for manufacturing and chronological dates. The chronology of the hoards included can be divided into two categories: two from the Early Iron Age and two from the Late Iron Age. The inclusion of Halstatt derivatives in the Llyn Fawr and Cardiff hoards plus native metal work pieces may indicate that the objects belonged to the indigenous inhabitants of Wales, who could have procured these objects by a variety of means.

Table 5 combines information from Llyn Fawr and Cardiff. As the table illustrates, when combining the two hoards, the majority of items are tools, followed by horse equipment, personal adornment objects, those used in the act of consumption and finally, weapons. The two hoards show that whilst the items included are predominantly constructed of bronze there are, however, a few inclusions of iron objects. These iron objects indicate the significance of the hoards especially as iron was very rare at this time. Objects made of iron would have been unusual and seen as special or precious, therefore, if these hoards were indeed offerings, they would have been particularly meaningful.

The Lesser Garth Hoard, though similar in date, differs from the Seven Sisters Hoard as most of the pieces in the former are made of iron, and include tools, production pieces and cauldron attachments. The pieces in the Seven Sisters Hoard are mostly constructed of bronze and consist of horse and items that would have been used in the production of objects, cauldron attachments, items of adornment and a single tool. The horse equipment from these two hoards is of a high quality and shows that single enamels as well as the application of the polychrome technique were being used.

The terret from Lesser Garth is inlayed with red enamel, a technique that is derived from southern England, although the terret is believed to be of local manufacture (Savory 1966). Some of the pieces of metal work from Seven Sisters have inclusions of polychrome enamel with white, yellow and blue inlay. This technique is datable to a Late Iron Age date, as the techniques used in this manufacturing process were not introduced to Britain until the Roman incursion of southern England.

Table 6 is a combination of the Pentyrch and Seven Sisters hoards; clearly pieces of horse equipment have become the predominant items far out-numbering tools (as in the earlier hoards). The objects included in the hoards at this time became highly ornamental and are decorated to a high standard suggesting that presentation of self had become an important theme. The items used in the consumption of food or drink has also risen indicating that ceremonial consumption of food and drink had also become an important part of life. The percentage of items used in bodily adornment fell slightly and the introduction of objects used in metal production is also present were introduced as opposed to the earlier hoards.

It has been suggested that the hoarding of objects is a result of tensions either from internal or external influence. Whatever the circumstances of deposition that surrounded the four hoards described here, a comparison of the inclusions in the early hoards, and those of the later period, illustrate that changes were taking place in the social and cultural ideology of the time. The Early and the Late Iron Age were times of great change and with change comes stress and worry; due to a fear of the unknown. Even though these hoards presented represent only a small percentage of those recorded from the whole of Wales, they illustrate that changes were occurring throughout the Iron Age. Whilst researching this chapter, it became apparent that there is a lack of synthesis and many gaps in the recent literature regarding hoard groups from across Britain. A comprehensive study of all hoard groups throughout Britain focusing on content, location and date is needed as this would be extremely beneficial to the understanding of the phenomena of hoarding during the Iron Age.

Table 1. Contents of the Llyn Fawr hoard.

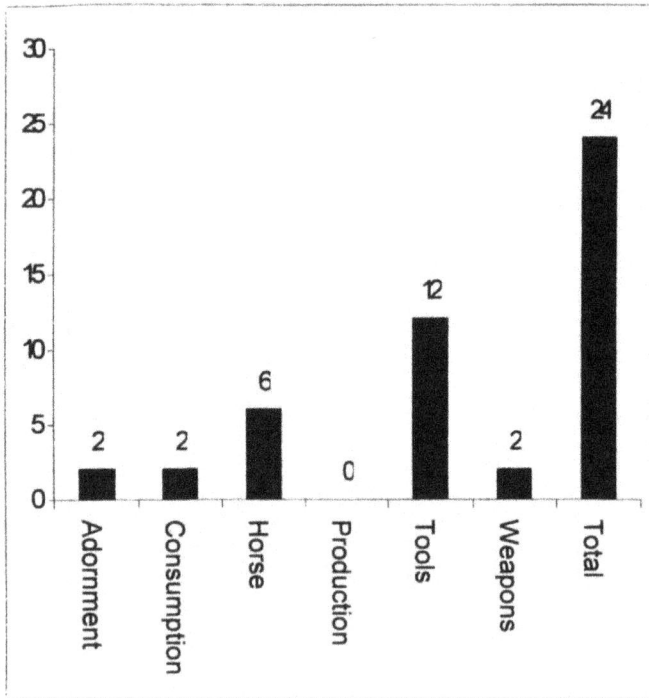

Table 2. Contents of the Cardiff Hoard

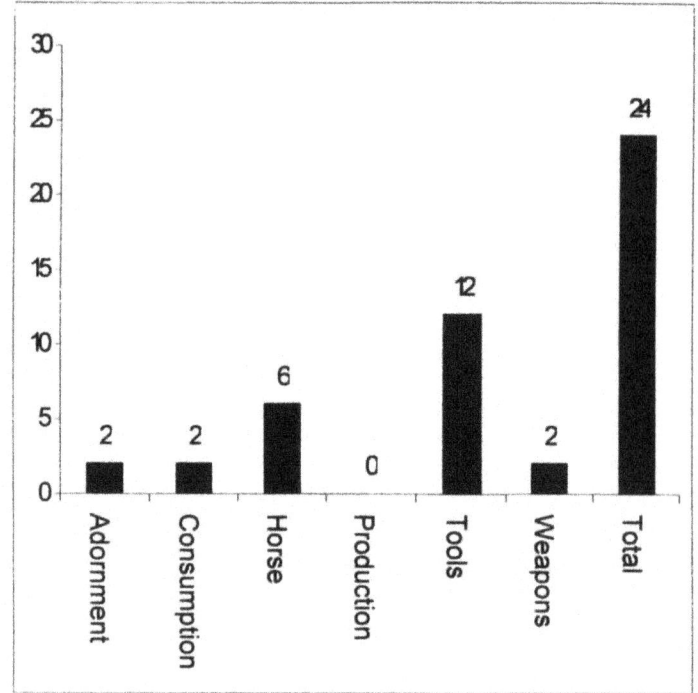

Table 3. Contents of the Seven Sister hoard.

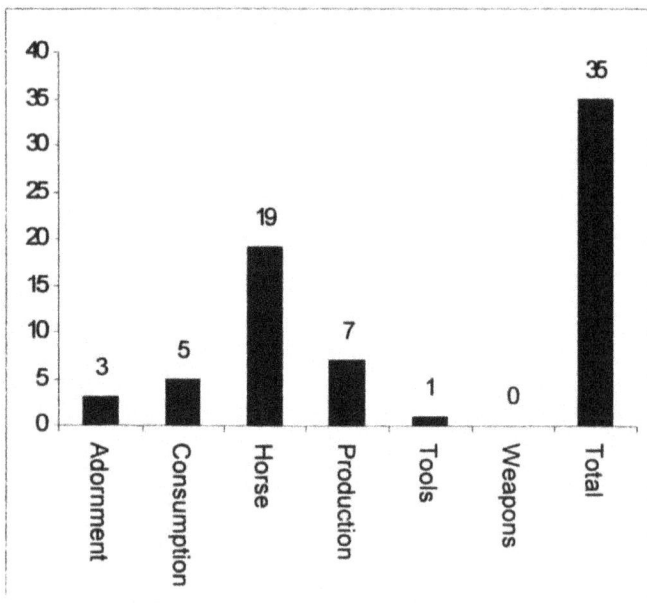

Table 4. Contents of Lesser Garth/Pentyrch.

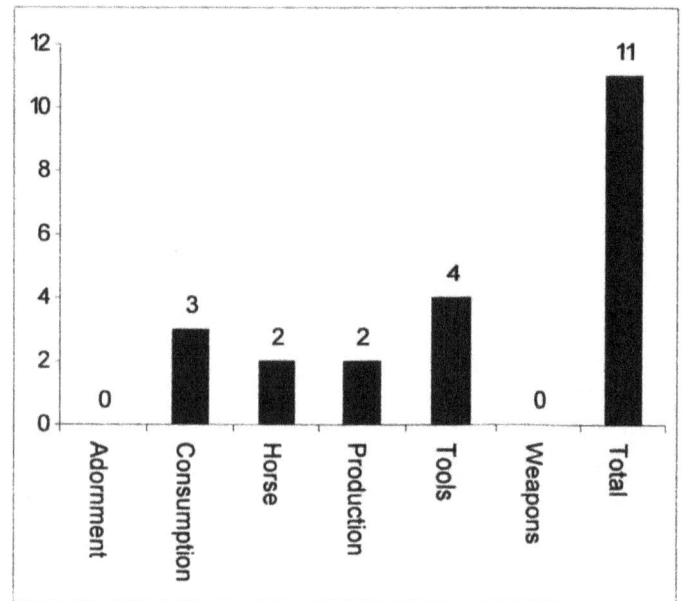

Chapter 6

Artefacts from Excavations

Within the Vale of Glamorgan and Gwent many Iron Age sites have been examined through excavation, these include hilltop enclosures such as Coed y Cymdda (Owen-John 1988), hillforts such as Castle Ditches/Llancarfan (Hogg 1976), Llanmelin (Nash-Williams 1933) and Twyn y Gaer (Probert 1976). Other sites to be discussed in this book include three Late Iron Age and Romano-British settlement sites at Caldicot (Vyner and Allen 1988), Whitton (Jarrett and Wrathmell 1981) and Biglis (Parkhouse 1988). Goldcliff (Bell *et al* 2000) and a number of other sites, namely Chapeltump and Magor Pill, which are situated along the Gwent Levels have recently been excavated and due to the preservation qualities of these wetland areas have produced a variety of datable material. Two caves have been recovered and excavated, these are Bacon Hole (Rutter 1948) and Minchin Hole (RCAHMW 1976a: 18) both have produced datable material culture. For the most part, where excavation has been undertaken, material culture in varying degrees has been recovered. The following chapter will discuss twenty sites from Gwent and Glamorgan where excavations have been carried out. There are many more sites that have not been included; the ones that have been, were chosen for their variability in type and in the material culture they have produced.

Structure of chapter

The structure will vary slightly in its format to that of the previous two chapters due to the substantial artefacts recovered, this makes it impossible to list them all within the confines of this book. A brief history of each site gives; the objects found will be discussed and where necessary, presented in tables according to the categories as outlined in the methodology. Whenever possible accession numbers associated with each assemblage are included and a full list of all items in each assemblage can be found in the appendix.

Index to excavated sites

Bacon Hole Cave, Penard – SS 5604 8682

This cave was first explored in 1850 by Colonel E. R. Wood. A number of Iron Age pottery sherds including the rim from an ovoid jar and a base fragment were recovered from this cave in 1919 and 1929 (Savory 1976: 69; Rutter 1948: 70, 74). Swansea Museum has made a reconstruction of the vessel and the sherds are housed in the National Museum and Gallery of Wales, Cardiff (RCAHMW 1976a: 18). There is evidence of occupation in the caves during the early prehistoric period and whilst there may be some doubt about domestic use of caves in the Bronze Age, the evidence for habitation during the Iron Age period is clear (RCAHMW 1976a: 10-21). Finds of a pre-Roman date are restricted to single bowls and metal objects at Culver Hole, Glamorgan (RCAHMW 1976a: 17), Minchin Hole (RCAHMW 1976a: 18) and Bacon Hole (RCAHMW 1976a: 18). The presence of hearths and domestic pottery at the caves found at Lesser Garth Cave (Hussey 1964-6) and metalworking activity at others caves such as Minchin Hole indicates that these caves were occupied for centuries beyond the Roman occupation of Wales (RCAHMW 1976b: 110).

Material culture

The fragments recovered from Bacon Hole are housed at the National Museum and Gallery of Wales, Cardiff.

Reconstructed bowl from Bacon Hole Cave. S.W.S: SM. 1939.78. See figure 66.

Collection of Iron Age pottery including rim fragment from ovoid jar with rounded, everted rim, plus a base fragment. N.M.W: 42.62.1. (Savory 1976: 69).

Biglis, Glamorgan - ST 142 940

Excavations carried out at Biglis by the Glamorgan-Gwent Archaeological trust in 1978-9 revealed the remains of a Late Iron Age Romano-British farmstead. Three main phases of activity were distinguished. The earliest phase of occupation began in the 1st century AD and consisted of an unenclosed group of huts that were probably circular in plan. This period of activity probably ended in the late 1st century AD, and the site was re-occupied in the latter part of the 2nd century AD when it was enclosed by a series of palisades. The site saw continual occupation until it was abandoned in the mid 4th century AD (Parkhouse 1988: 7). Although the earliest phase of occupation could not be precisely dated, the characteristics of the finds from the features were sherds of pottery of a calcite-gritted native fabric, some of which is decorated in the Glastonbury tradition, therefore a suggested date ((Webster 1988: 33) of the beginning of the 1st century AD is proposed for this phase at Bigliss.

Material culture

The material culture recovered from Biglis is housed at The National Museum and Gallery, Cardiff.

Complete bone point, manufactured from a sheep metapodial. This type of manufactured point is a well-known form and is most common in an Iron Age or later context. Often interpreted as gouges (Wheeler 1943: 303-6) or awls, they are perhaps better described as pin-beaters (Crowfoot 1945). This type of object, however, may have been used in a number of ways. (Greep 1988: 57, fig 41, 58). N.M.W: 82.68.H.2. See figure 67.

A pennanular brooch in poor condition. The terminals are at right angles to the plane of the ring. This type of pennanular brooch is classified as Fowlers type D, dated from the 1st century BC to the 3rd century AD (Fowler 1960, 151, fig 1; 152, 176). This brooch was recovered from boundary bank rubble (Webster 1988: 53; 55 fig 5). N.M.W: 82.68.H.2. See figure 68.

A pennanular brooch classified as a Fowlers class D1 and dated from 1st to the 3rd centuries AD. Examples of this type of brooch have been found at Caerleon and Glamorgan; this specimen was recovered from a palisade trench (Fowler 1960: 151, fig 1; 152, 176; Webster 1988: 53; 55, fig 6). N.M.W: 82.68.H.2. See figure 69.

The lower leg, part of the foot and part of the catch plate of a brooch, possibly a Hod Hill derivative (Brailsford 1962, fig 10; Webster 1988: 53; 55 fig 8). This example was found in plough soil.

Caldicot - ST 464 975

Early in 1976, Mr. D. Tucker of Caerwent discovered a silver coin of Dobunnic issue in association with sherds of native and Romano-British pottery in topsoil that was being removed in an extension to Caerwent Quarry. The finds prompted a trial excavation that was carried out by the Glamorgan-Gwent Archaeological trust in 1977 (Vyner and Allen 1988: 67). Five phases of activity were distinguished ranging from the pre-Roman period to the 4th century AD. In the earliest phase, a number of finds are markedly earlier than any evidence for settlement. In the absence of any early structures, the finds evidence is enough to allow assumption of a Late Iron Age or earlier occupation of Caldicot.

Material culture

The material culture recovered from Caldicot is housed at The National Museum and Gallery, Cardiff; the author has no record of the accession numbers.

Silver coin, Dobunni inscribed [EISV], divided EI and SV above and below a three-tailed horse to R on the reverse; slightly worn (Boon 1988: 91; Mack 1975).

One-piece bow brooch, La Tène III, dated 1st century BC. This type of brooch has a predominantly West Country distribution there are known examples from Glastonbury, Somerset (Bullied and Gray 1911-17, i: 195-7) and Hod Hill, Dorset (Richmond 1968) This brooch is misshapen possibly arising from repair or damage (Boon 1988: 93; 94 fig 1). See figure 70.

Bow brooch, Hod Hill type, La Tène III, dated 1st century BC, with hinged pin, formerly tin-plated. Shows signs of repair, originally tin-plated but an addition or repair has been added the exact shape and purpose not clear (Boon 1988: 93; 94 fig 2). See figure 71.

La Tène III brooch, no trace of tinning or repairs, pin missing (Boon 1988: 93; 94 fig 3). See figure 72.

Fragment La Tène III brooch (Boon 1988: 93; 94 fig 4). See figure 73.

Pennanular brooch with moulded bent-back terminals. Similar to pieces found at Hod Hill (Brailsford 1962); Bagendon (Clifford 1961) and South Cadbury (Alcock 1972: 72 pl 66), dated to the 1st century (Robinson page 93 item 8; 94 fig 8). See figure 74.

Fragmentary, one-piece iron brooch, La Tène III. Commonly found in southern and central England but rarely in the west of England and Wales. Parallels are found at Hengistbury Head (Bushe-Fox 1915) and Camulodunum (Hawkes and Hull 1947: 308-9), dated to the 1st century BC (Boon 1988: 98, fig 30; 99 item 30). See figure 75.

Complete iron pennanular brooch ; similar type recovered from Hod Hill (Brailsford 1962: fig 11; Boon 1988: 98 fig 31; 99 item 31). See figure 76.

Part of a Kimmeridge Shale (Sunter and Woodward 1987) bracelet. The pattern design on this example suggests it is pre-Roman in origin, comparable to examples from Glastonbury (Bullied and Gray 1911-17, i, 258-9; Boon 1988: 99).

Chapeltump, Goldcliff and Magor Pill

The Welsh Severn Estuary has one of the greatest concentrations of prehistoric intertidal archaeology found in Britain. A number of sites have been investigated by Martin Bell, Astrid Caseldine and Heike Neumann (2000). Evidence for Iron Age activity is concentrated at Goldcliff, although further evidence of activity has been identified during a survey at Cold Harbour Pill-2 where palaeochannels contained a line of round wood verticals and a woven structure thought to relate to fishing activity. Iron Age pottery and a single wooden post had previously been recorded in a palaeochannels at Magor Pill (Whittle 1989). Other Iron Age material culture has been recorded from the palaeochannels at Chapeltump-4 and from a trackway at Chapeltump-5 (Bell et al 2000: 317-8).

Material culture

The material recovered from Goldcliff, Chapeltump and Magor is housed at Newport Museum and the National Museum and Gallery of Wales, Cardiff.

Goldcliff-ST 377 823

Iron Age timber posts. N.M.W: 98.24.H.
Waterlogged wood and other structural material, C-14 dated to 4th century to 1st century BC and includes re-used Bronze Age boat plank. N.P.T: 90.109.

Chapeltump- ST 445 851

Pottery body sherds, black shell gritted ware. N.P.T: 94.161.3.

Iron Age pottery sherds. N.M.W: 86.55.H.1.

Coed y Cymdda, Near Wenvoe, South Glamorgan – ST 1329 7398

Excavations of this hill-slope enclosure were carried out by the Glamorgan-Gwent Archaeological trust between 1978-1980. The enclosure is a sub-rectangular, univallate earthwork with an internal area of c. 5000 square metres. Seven phases of activity were distinguishable from the excavated evidence these range from the Late Mesolithic to the Roman period (Owen-John 1988: 73, 76). Although some of the material recovered has been dated to the Iron Age, an exact date for the Iron Age horizon is difficult to establish due to the lack of structural evidence.

Material culture

The material culture recovered from Coed y Cymmda is housed at The National Museum and Gallery, Cardiff.

Domestic Production

In this category are a variety of utilised stones such as hearthstones, potboilers, a rotary quern stone, whetstones, and slingstones. N.M.W: 91.2. H.66 through to N.M.W: 91.2. H.105.

Pottery

The Iron Age pottery comes from a broad based handmade barrel-shaped jar, with flattened rim fragments, dated to c.300-50 BC (Owen-John 1988). N.M.W: 91.2.H.61. through to N.M.W: 91.2. H.62.

Production

A number of pieces of good quality iron ore, weighing in total 770 g and a nodule of haematite weighing 170 g, were recovered from a variety of contexts. N.M.W: 91.2.H.106 through to N.M.W: 91.2.H.123. N.M.W: 91.2.H.77. N.M.W: 91.2.H.79.

Weapons

A number of slingstones were collected during excavation and they have been included in this section as a form of weapon. N.M.W: 91.2.H.89 through to N.M.W: 91.2.H.91.

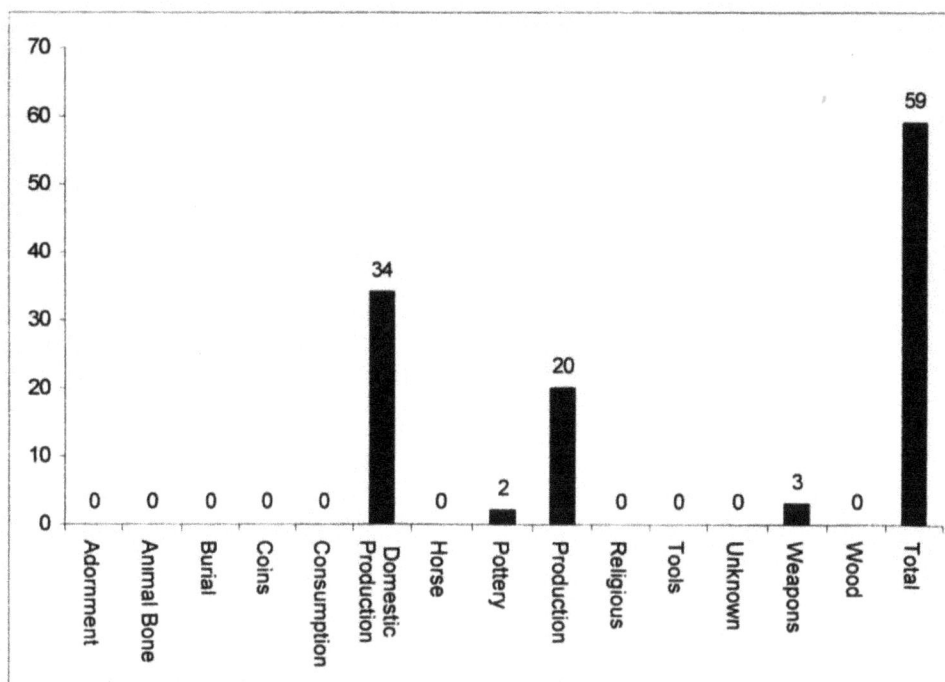

Table 7. Ratios of material culture recovered from Coed y Cymdda.

Harding's Down – SS 434 908

Harding's Down is a multivallate hillfort and is one of three in this vicinity. This hillfort was initially a simple univallate enclosure. The outer ramparts were a later unfinished addition (Hogg 1973). Hogg excavated here in the last two weeks of October 1962, sectioning the ramparts and clearing the entrance and two hut-platforms. The excavation revealed that the entrance was cobbled with stone lined sides; the presence of large postholes in the entranceway indicates that four large posts would have supported double gates (Whittle 1992: 32-2). A small quantity of plain pottery was recovered from here of a mid Iron Age date (Whittle 1992: 33). Parallels for the pottery can been found at Llanmelin (Nash-Williams 1933) and Sudbrook (Nash-Williams 1933). Also recovered was an iron wedge of unknown use plus pounding and rubbing stones and a small amount of iron slag from the bottom of a bowl furnace (Hogg 1973).

Material culture

The material culture recovered from Harding's Down is housed at The National Museum and Gallery, Cardiff; accession numbers are only available for a number of the listed items.

Fragments of pottery. N.M.W: 83.31.1.

Slag from the bottom of bowl furnace. N.M.W: unknown.

Iron wedge. N.M.W: unknown.

Pounding and rubbing stones. N.M.W: unknown.

High Penard Promontory Fort – SS 567 866

High Penard is a small-defended site protected by cliffs on all sides except for the north and north-east, where two artificial ramparts have been constructed (Whittle 1992: 52-3). Postholes discovered in 1939 by Audrey Williams revealed that the entranceway was blocked by a pair of gates (Williams 1941). Within the rampart was a rock cut gully leading to a pit; the purpose of this gully is unclear but it has been suggested that it represents an early system for the collection of water (Williams 1939: 26). Evidence of occupation was found in the interior indicating a mixed economy of farming, fishing and hunting. The site was in use in the Late Iron Age and continued to be occupied until around the 2nd century AD.

Material culture

The material culture recovered from High Penard is housed at The National Museum and Gallery, Cardiff; the author has no record of the accession numbers.

A few pottery sherds. N.M.W: unknown.

A spindle whorl. N.M.W: unknown.

Daub fragments. N.M.W: unknown.

Castle Ditches/ Llancarfan – SS 960 674

Castle Ditches/Llancarfan was excavated by Hogg in 1963 and 1964 and is a large univallate hillfort situated in the Vale of Glamorgan. The entranceway of this site is partly inturned and beneath the entranceway is a trace of a wall thought to be part of an earlier enclosure constructed no earlier than c. 4th century BC. The hillfort at Harding's Down was constructed no earlier than c. 2nd century BC (Whittle 1992: 31).

Material culture

The material culture recovered from Castle Ditches/Llancarfan is housed at The National Museum and Gallery, Cardiff; the author has no record of the accession numbers.

Adornment

From pre-Roman levels a brooch spring with nine coils and a two-piece of wire were recovered. N.M.W: unknown.

A bronze nail cleaner, Roman in appearance, was found in association with a fragment of a moratorium rim, three scraps of Samian Ware and four sherds of coarse pottery. N.M.W: 84.33.H.3. See figure 77.

Animal bones (see table 8)

A substantial amount of animal bones was recovered during excavation; the ratios of which are shown in table 8. Over 526 specimens were found, of which, only 256 were identifiable. Only one complete skeleton was found, that of an immature lamb showing no signs of butchery. Other animals, about a quarter of which were sheep, were killed whilst young, and the remainder of the bones are from mature animals. There are no butchering marks on the bones; this may be due, however, to the fragmentary state of the bones retrieved. The evidence from the excavated area suggests that no one area had any noticeable accumulations of animal bone; all appear to be evenly distributed (Hogg 1977: 38-9). N.M.W: Unknown.

Table 8. Animals represented at Castle Ditches/Llancarfan.

Animal	Bones	Teeth	Animal Total
Sheep/Goat	87	71	30
Cattle	94	56	30
Pig	35	5	20
Dog	11	1	5
Horse	17	12	10
Deer	12	6	10
Bird	2	0	2

Burial

One human skeleton was recovered from Llancarfan it is one of the few possible Iron Age burials recorded from Wales. The skeleton is thought to be a female aged around twenty-five years old was recovered from within a small bowl-shaped hollow that had been dug into a ditch filling. The head and arms of the skeleton are damaged, possibly due to the corpse being pressed forcibly into the small hollow. Examination of the tibia shows a squatting facet indicating that this woman spent a lot of time in a squatting position. Unusual features of this skeleton show a congenital deformity to the spinal column; the second and third cervical vertebrae were fused (Hogg 1977: 38). A number of skeletons from this period show signs of unusual abnormalities. For example, the hand phalanges of Lindow I and III had an abnormality, indicating the presence of two short finger digits (Brothwell & Bourke 1995: 56). Another example is the skeleton of a young man recovered from one of the pits at Danebury whose skeletal remains indicate that in life the young man had a deformed hip, probably caused by Perthes Disease, a disorder that afflicts young children (Hooper 1984: 463-74). N.M.W: Unknown.

Domestic Production

A single half-bun shaped loom weight of baked clay was recovered from the top of one of the ramparts. N.M.W: Unknown.

A single spindle whorl was also recovered. N.M.W: Unknown.

Horse

A bronze harness ring (for full discussion of this item see Hogg 1972: 30) found inside the gateway of the early stone walled fort in association with a number of iron fragments (see production below *). See figure 78. N.M.W: 84.33.H.2.

Pottery

Nine sherds of decorated pottery were recovered representing approximately four pots, consistent with pottery recovered from Glastonbury (Bulleid and Gray 1911). A number of coarse pottery fragments were also recovered that share characteristics with pottery found at Croft Ambrey (Stanford 1974) but are more likely to belong to the Lydney-Llanmelin group (Cunliffe 1974: 43-4). N.M.W: Unknown.

Production

A lump of slag from the bottom of a furnace indicates that iron was being manufactured here. Pieces were found in many areas and levels suggesting that the amount of metalwork activity on the site, overall, must have been considerable. In addition to the slag, lumps of clay with traces of slag adhering were found. These fragments were originally thought to be pieces of daub but it would be more plausible to consider them sections of a furnace, however, this cannot be verified until scientifically analysed is conducted. There is evidence that bronze was also being worked at this site but to a lesser degree than iron. A number of unidentifiable iron fragments were recovered. * A harness ring was recovered in association with a number of metal objects believed to be fragments of a chariot or cart (Hogg 1977: 28-9). A number of iron nails and a small variety of tools were also recovered.

Scrap of an iron blade. N.M.W: unknown.

Four iron bars of various lengths. N.M.W: unknown.

Iron plate. N.M.W: unknown.

Three iron nails. N.M.W: unknown.

Four fragments of iron blades. N.M.W: unknown.

Variety of iron spikes bars and strips. N.M.W: unknown.

Iron hook. N.M.W: unknown.

Iron stud. N.M.W: unknown.

Five broken iron Nails. N.M.W: unknown.

Tools

A variety of tools were recovered during excavation including a chisel, an awl, an iron spike and a number of knife blades. N.M.W: unknown

Weapons

Twenty-nine sling stones. N.M.W: unknown.

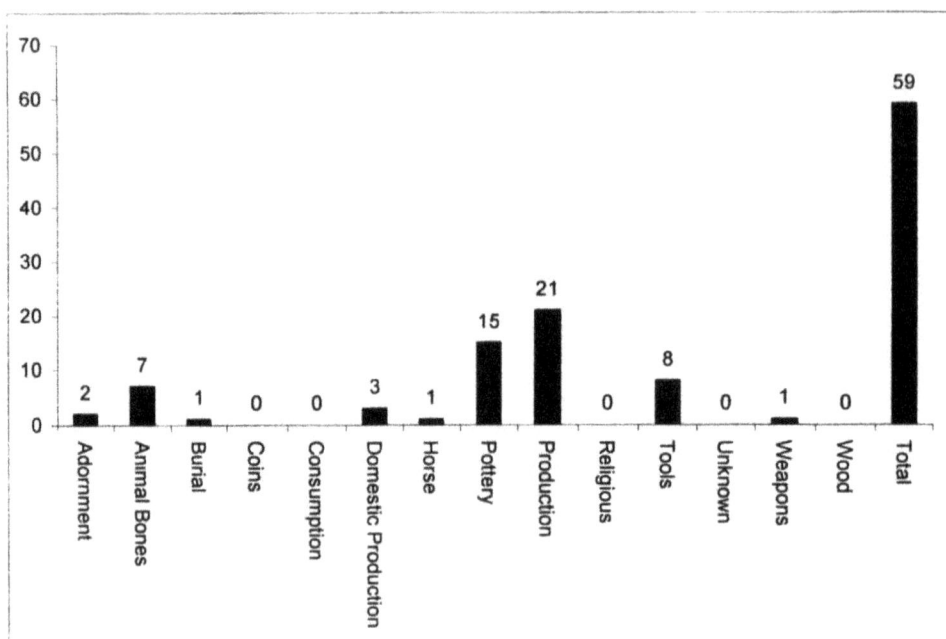

Table 9. Ratios of Material Culture from Castle Ditches/Llancarfan.

Llanmelin - ST 461 926

Llanmelin is a small multivallate hillfort comprised of two main parts. One part is an elliptical enclosure measuring approximately 228 meters by 152 meters, with an internal radius of nearly 5 ½ acres, attached to the ellipse is an area of about 2 ½ acres that is located on one of the longer sides. The second part is a narrow, oblong annexe that measures approximately 121 metres by 70 metres wide (Nash-Williams 1933). Excavations were conducted at Llanmelin by Nash-William from 1930 to 1932 and the excavations revealed that the main enclosure is surrounded by two, and in some places three, large, well-preserved banks which are at their highest near the partly inturned entrance (Whittle 1992: 48-9). To the south-east of the main enclosure, there are a series of outer, small banks that are tacked on to form a

number of annexes. These are sub-rectangular in shape and only show signs of one entranceway. The excavations revealed that Llanmelin originated sometime in the 3rd century BC when only a smaller enclosure existed that was surrounded by a single bank and ditch. These features have become obscured by the later banks, however, small traces of the single bank and ditch are visible outside the main enclosure on the north-east side near the outpost. This outpost is a small c-shaped enclosure with a double bank that lies in a woodland area about 200 metres to the north of the main enclosure and is thought to be contemporary with the earliest phases of Llanmelin. The main multivallate enclosure at Llanmelin was constructed around 150 BC but no substantial evidence for settlement inside the ramparts was found during excavation for this period. The final phase here, which began *c.* 50 BC, involved the remodelling and strengthening of the entrance, perhaps to protect the inhabitants of the hillfort, suggesting an increased threat of attack. The north-east side of the main enclosure was cut back and refaced and both sides were given flanking timber platforms and palisades on top of the banks. The entranceway was protected by a wooden gate at the inner end. The annexes were added during this phase, possibly for the corralling of animals, as there was no sign of human occupation in the excavated areas of the annexes. The fort was abandoned *c.* 75. AD (Whittle 1992: 49; Nash-Williams). There are traces of intensive occupation at four separate points on this site: inside the south-western and north-eastern defences, on a workshop floor within the camp, and on both sides of the entranceway (Nash-Williams 1933: 289-291).

Material culture

The material culture recovered from Llanmelin is housed at The National Museum and Gallery, Cardiff.

Adornment

Bronze pennanular brooch with spiral terminals with the pin missing. A parallel was found at Glastonbury (Bulleid and Gray 1911; Nash-Williams 1933: 308 item 1; 306 figure 1). See figure 79. N.M.W: 31.345.1 (i).

Fragments of bronze bracelets with a ribbed decoration. Parallels recovered from Hengistbury Head (Bushe-Fox 1915; Cunliffe 1978; 1987). N.M.W: 31.345.17. See figure 80.

Animal Bones

A number of fragmentary animal remains were recovered during excavation including bones of oxen, horse, pig, dog, sheep or goat and red deer. All the animal bones are incomplete and in a very fragmentary state (Cowley, in Nash-Williams 1933: 310). N.M.W: unknown.

Burials

The human remains consist of the bones of two individuals. One of these is a male aged between 25 and 40 years of age.

The skull is badly damaged but has been reconstructed, and the teeth are well worn. Due to the incomplete nature of the long bones, no description of the stature of this individual is available. It has been suggested that the second set of skeletal remains belong to that of a female of uncertain age; the skull is missing but some of the long bones are complete. Inspection of these show that at their distal ends, the tibias show facets that indicate that, in life, this person spent a lot of time in a squatting position (Cowley in Nash-Williams 1933: 310). N.M.W: unknown. See figure 81.

Pottery

The pottery recovered during excavation falls into four categories:

Handmade jars of the 'flower pot' type made of coarse ware varying from grey-black to light brown in colour. Decoration, where present, is of incised chevrons, wavy and eyebrow patterns. This group shows close affinities to pottery at Glastonbury (Bullied and Gray 1911) and in its earliest form dates to the 2nd century BC (Nash-Williams 1939: 289).

High-shouldered, bead-rimmed jars, examples are both handmade and thrown by a wheel with the colours varying from hard grey to buff white. It has been suggested that the vessels show Belgic influence and are dated to between 45-75 AD (Nash-Williams 1933: 289).

The third and fourth categories are both Roman and medieval in provenance

Pottery

N.M.W: 31.30.2 through to N.M.W: 31.31.20.

N.M.W: 31.345.1 through to N.M.W: 31.345.43.

N.M.W: 77.1.

N.M.W: 32.385.1 through to N.M.W: 32.385.46.

For detailed description of all the pottery recovered during excavation, see (Nash-Williams 1939: 291-307).

Production

Evidence of metalworking can be seen by the presence of a crucible and iron slag, other items in this section include iron ties, iron shanks and quartz.

Iron tie. N.M.W: 31.345.44.

Triangular crucible fragments. N.M.W: 31.345.7.

Binding fragment. N.M.W: 31.345.8.

Iron slag. N.M.W: 31.30.15.

Thin piece of flint ground and polished. N.M.W: 32.385.21.

An iron shank. N.M.W: 32.385.23.

Iron slag. N.M.W: 32.385.26.

Iron slag. N.M.W: 32.385.42.

Iron slag. N.M.W: 32.385.44.

Iron slag. N.M.W: 32.385.46.

Piece of quartz. N.M.W: 32.385.47.

Tools

Tine deer knife handle. N.M.W: unknown.

Unknown

These two items are of unknown classification and of

unknown material in appearance and texture they resemble black plastic but could be channel coal. N.M.W: 31.345.16. N.M.W: 32.385.16.

Weapons

The only items found that can be classified as weapons are slingstones. N.M.W:32.385.48.

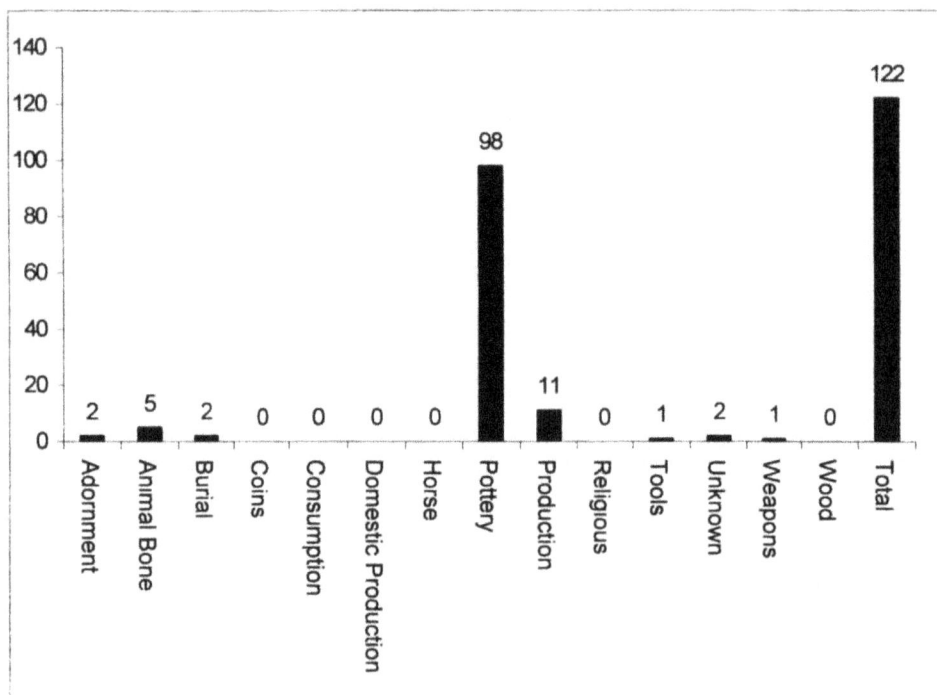

Table 10. Ratios of Material Culture from Llanmelin.

Lodge Wood - ST 323 913

A small-scale excavation was conducted here by Dr Ray Howell and Dr Joshua Pollard from the University of Wales College, Newport in the summer of 2000. A number of trenches were placed in the interior of a small oval enclosure at the centre of the fort, across the western entrance and across the southern inner defences. The trench in the interior revealed a rectangular posthole structure and a shallow number of Middle Iron Age pottery sherds (report forthcoming Pollard & Howell). Thanks are offered to Dr J Pollard and Dr R Howell who gave their permission for a drawing of the brooch to be included in this book (Gwilt 2002: 2-3; Howell and Pollard 2000 AIW 40:81-3). Items held at University Wales College, Newport.

Material culture

The material culture from the excavations is held at the University of Wales College, Newport. The report for this excavation is forthcoming.

La Téne I Brooch. See figure 82. Unknown.

Middle Iron Age pottery. Unknown.

Marlborough Grange – SS 973 735

Collection of pottery, of a Late Bronze Age or very Early Iron Age date, found during excavations in 1967 in the upper filling of a quarry on the south side of a Bronze Age round cairn at Marlborough Grange, Llanblethian (Savory 1969: 49-72; Savory 1976: 55). Most of the sherds are from a large bucket-shaped jar with flaring rim and a finger printed cordon. Pottery sherds. N.M.W: 68.311.17.

Material culture

The material culture recovered from the site is housed at The National Museum and Gallery, Cardiff.

Animal Bones

A number of fragmentary animal bones and teeth were recovered during the excavation including bones of oxen, immature horse, pig, the lower jaw of a dog, sheep or goat. All the animal bones are incomplete and in a very fragmentary state (Matheson in Fox 1929: 63-4).

A collection of animal bones and teeth. (Savory 1976: 67). N.M.W: 27.66.19.

Flint, shells and 114 animal teeth (Figgis 2000: 54-61).S.W.S: A903.11

Domestic Production

Bronze perforated disc (small) with broken shank, possibly from the foot of a brooch (Savory 1976: 68, 75). N.M.W: 54.19.2

Adornment (Merthyr Mawr)

Unfinished spindle whorl. (Savory 1976: 67). N.M.W: 27.66.1.

Hearth fragments. S.W.S: A903.5.7

Fragment of the upper part of a beehive quern made of coarse grit. N.M.W: 35.526.

Electrum twisted silver wire bracelet. N.M.W: 29.447.

Potboilers and hearthstones. N.M.W: 26.239.30.

Bronze brooch, La Tène I type, which was recovered in 1929 (Fox 1929: 146-7; Savory 1976: 67). The brooch belongs to the Hull and Hawkes Group 1A. (Hull and Hawkes 1987: Page 84 plate 26: 3383). N.M.W: 29.208. See figure 83.

Iron ring headed-pin. N.M.W: 26.239.2. See figure 82.

Pottery

Very little pottery was recovered, included was fine-gritted ware with well-smoothed grey buff surface, rim from ovoid jar with beaded rim.

Undistinguishable pottery sherds

Bronze La Téne I Brooch, six coiled spring. N.M.W: 26.239.1. (Savory 1976: 68, 75). N.M.W: 54.1

Merthyr Mawr – SS 862 768

Merthyr Mawr Warren is an example of an open coastal settlement. The evidence collected from this site suggests recurrent occupation that was interrupted by episodes of be-sanding. The area was involved in metalworking activities as can be seen by the material culture recovered from here. Disappointingly, only a very small-scale excavation was carried out by C. Fox during 1926. A number of sections were cut across three mounds that showed evidence of human occupation. The following represents the material culture recovered during 1926.

Material Culture

The material culture recovered from Merthyr Mawr is housed at the National Museum and Gallery, Cardiff and Swansea Museum

Fragment of handmade pottery, unknown type. (Savory 1976: 67). N.M.W: 27.66.2.

Tools

Axe-head. S.W.S: A903.5.1 (Figgis 2000: 54-61).

Axe-head. S.W.S: A903.5.2 (Figgis 2000: 54-61).

Knife. S.W.S: A903.5.3 (Figgis 2000: 54-61).

Production

A lot of debris from a variety of manufacturing processes is visible at Merthyr Mawr they include:

Corroded iron nail. N.M.W: 26.239.3.

Fragments of crucibles of grey ware hard and vitrified, with drops of bronze still adhering to it. N.M.W: 26.239.4 through N.M.W: 26.239.14.

Iron slag fragments. N.M.W: 26.239.15.

Fragments of an iron plate. N.M.W: 26.239.16 and N.M.W: 26.239.17.Fragments of fused bronze. N.M.W: 26.239.18

Strips of bronze strip. N.M.W: 26.239.25 and N.M.W: 26.239.26.

Fragments of bronze. N.M.W: 26.239.27.

Minute bronze nail. N.M.W: 26.239.28.

Piece of flat-sectioned wire bent in the shape of a diamond. N.M.W: 26.239.29.

Fragments of bronze smelting crucibles, all made from hard grey ware. (Savory 1976: 67). N.M.W: 27.66.3 through to N.M.W: 27.66.15.

Iron fragments. (Savory 1976: 67). N.M.W: 27.66.16.

A number of jets, drops and fragments of bronze. (Savory 1976: 67). N.M.W: 27.66.17.

Number of iron slag fragments. (Savory 1976: 67). N.M.W: 27.66.18.

A collection of shells. (Savory 1976: 67). N.M.W: 27.66.20.

A round sectioned bronze ring. (Savory 1976: 67). N.M.W: 28.485.

Crucible fragments. (Savory 1976: 68). N.M.W: 47.164.73.

Bronze fragments. (Savory 1976: 68). N.M.W: 47.164.74.

Iron ore fragments. (Savory 1976: 68). N.M.W: 47.164.75.

Nails. S.W.S: A903.5.4

Nails. S.W.S: A903.5.5

Iron slag. S.W.S: A903.5.6

Bronze droplets. S.W.S: A903.5.8.

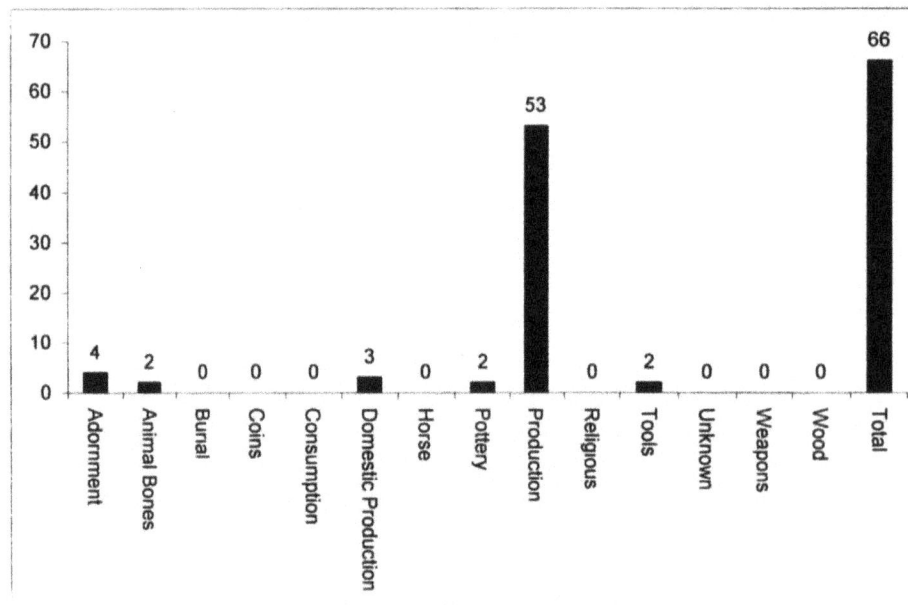

Table 11. Ratios of Material Culture from Merthyr Mawr Warren excavations.

Mynydd Bychan – SS 963 757

Mynydd Bychan is a small, sub-triangular, multivallate enclosure. Internally the site measures approximately fifty-eight metres by forty-six metres; the whole area measures roughly just less than half an acre. Even though the site is small, it is strongly defended. The site was excavated during 1949 and 1950 by Savory (1954; 1955) and the excavations revealed that there had been three phases of occupation.

Phase I: c.50 BC to 50 AD. This phase saw the construction of the defences around a group of timber-framed circular huts; it ended with the rapid decay or more likely, the demolition of the defences, and perhaps with the burning of the structures, although this is uncertain.

Phase II: *c.* 50 AD to 100 AD. This phase saw the construction within the ruined defences of a new phase of occupation, consisting of three round houses that had dry-stone wall foundations set inside courtyards. The material evidence suggests that the site was abandoned and was not reoccupied until the 11th century AD.

Phase III: c. 11th to 13th centuries AD. This is not discussed here.

Material culture
The material culture recovered from Merthyr Mawr is housed at The National Museum and Gallery, Cardiff.

Adornment

Spiral bronze finger-ring made from a strip that is widest at its centre and coiled to give a flattened, elliptical bezel with an engraved decoration of two converging tramlines. N.M.W: 32.46.1.

Spiral bronze finger-ring, made from a strip that is widest at its centre, it has no decoration. N.M.W: 49.418.1. See figure 85.

Bronze pennanular brooch with the pin missing (Savory 1976: 72). Found in an unstratified context. The terminals appear to be pinched back but on closer inspection, one can see that they were cast and later tooled to give the appearance of a fold. This is a Pre-Roman type that persisted into the Roman period. This brooch belongs to the second phase at Mynydd Bychan, contemporary with the pottery and is similar in form to one recovered from Culver Hole Cave (Savory 1949-50). N.M.W: 49.418.2.

Link from a bronze chain, made from circular section wire. N.M.W: 49.418.3.

Iron strip bow brooches, the pins are missing and they both have cylindrical heads, believed to be of the Roman

Conquest period. *c.* 1st century AD. N.M.W. 49.418.4 and N.M.W: 49.418.5.

Iron bow brooch with the catch plate and most of the pin is missing; found with burial on north of main ditch in IE (Savory 1976: 72). N.M.W: 49.418.6.

Four fragments of iron brooches (Savory 1976: 72). N.M.W: 49.418.7

Possible iron coil from the spring of a brooch. N.M.W: 49.418.8

Badly corroded iron bow brooch with no catch plate. Found in third disturbed burial on north lip of main ditch in section IE (Savory 1949-50: 41 item 3; Savory 1976: 72). NMW: unknown.

Possible fragment of brooch. N.M.W: 50.297.

Animal Bones

A number of animal bones consisting of broken teeth and bones were recovered from Phases I and II at Mynydd Bychan. These include oxen, sheep, pig, horse, dog, fox, short-tailed field vole, and a possible swan (Cowley in Savory 1955: 50). N.M.W: 49.418.45.

Burials

Human remains recovered from here represent three individuals. The bones are in a very fragmentary state and no human skulls were recovered. The remains are as follows:

An adult male skeleton. The bones are robust in appearance.

A young female skeleton. The remains of a partial skull were recovered as well as parts of the lower jaw, in which the teeth were worn down.

An adult of uncertain gender. The remains of this individual were too fragmentary to determine the sex (Cowley in Savory 1955: 49). N.M.W: 49.418.45.

Domestic Production

Five spindle whorls were recovered, two are simple disc shaped whorls and show similarities to some found at Glastonbury (Bulleid and Gray 1911: 582) and Maiden Castle, (Wheeler 1943), and two are spheroid in shape and are also represented at Glastonbury (Savory 1955: 45-6).

Five spindle whorls. N.M.W: 49.418.38 through to N.M.W: 49.418.42.

Two fragments of beehive rotary querns were also recovered. N.M.W: 49.418.43 and N.M.W: 49.418.44.

Pottery

Pottery recovered from Mynydd Bychan is represented by only a few rim fragments; no complete vessels were found. Reconstruction drawings illustrate that the fragments represent well-finished, small, handmade jars or bowls of either a grey or a brown fabric with white specks of grit included. These simple forms are typical of local groups of pottery from Wessex and the Cotswolds and Monmouthshire and are thought to represent a local industry (Savory 1955: 34-40). The pottery recovered from Phase II at Mynydd Bychan is also native in provenance, however, it is in marked contrast to that from Phase I as these fragments were wheel-turned and are constructed of finer material. Most of the material has been fired to an orange/brick colour sometimes leaving a bluish-grey centre. These forms are generally of a Late Iron Age date (Savory 1955: 38) with parallels found at Sudbrook and Caerleon.

Iron Age pottery. N.M.W: 49.418.13. through to N.M.W: 49.418.20.

Iron Age pottery. N.M.W: 49.418.21. through to N.M.W: 49.418.36.

Fragments of pottery sherds. N.M.W: 50.297.4 through to N.M.W: 50.297.8

Production

Evidence of metalworking activity is present on this site in the form of a quantity of iron slag (Howard in Savory 1955: 48-9).

Fragments of iron strip and sheeting: N.M.W: 49.418.12.

Four pieces of iron ore. N.M.W: 49.418.45.

Fragments of iron strip and sheeting: N.M.W: 50.297.3.

Tools

Tools represented are made in a variety of materials including bone borers and gouges, an iron file, awl and an iron ox-goad tip.

An iron awl. N.M.W: 49.418. 9.

Iron ox-goad tip. N.M.W: 49.418. 10.

An iron file. N.M.W: 49.418. 11.

Fragments of worked bone. N.M.W: 49.418. 37.

Weapons

Large quantities of slingstones were found in two hoards: one pile of 150 and another of 40. N.M.W: 50.297.9.

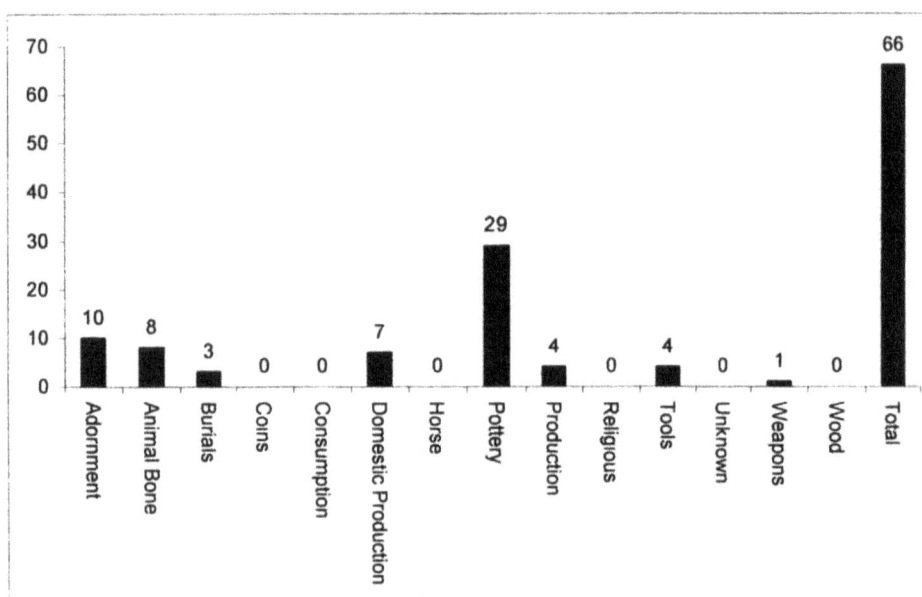

Table 12. Ratio of material culture from Mynydd Bychan excavation.

Porthkerry Promontory Fort at Bulwalks – ST 082 664

This is a large multivallate earthwork situated on the coast, one and a half miles or 0.8 kilometers west-south-west from Barry in the Vale of Glamorgan (Gardner 1935). Two excavations have been carried out here; the first in 1935 by Gardner and the second during 1968 by Davies (1973). The later excavation revealed three rectangular buildings behind the innermost rampart. The earliest is undated and the other two date from the 1st to 2nd centuries AD and the 3rd and 4th centuries AD. Postholes were found positioned in the

entranceway indicating that this site was sealed by double gates (Davies 1938; Whittle 1992: 51-2). The finds recovered indicate that a mixed economy was practiced at this site.

The material culture recovered from the Porthkerry Promontory Fort is housed at The National Museum and Gallery, Cardiff.

Material culture

Only a few sherds of small-undecorated body fragments are represented. The fabric varies in colour from dark grey to fawn. Parallels for the sherds, in terms of their fabrics, can be found at other Iron Age sites in Glamorgan, such as: Llancarfan (Castle Ditches), Caer Dynnaf and Cae Summerhouse (Davies 1973: 85-98). N.M.W; Unknown.

The Knave Promontory Fort, Rhossili, Glamorgan – SS 432 864

This site, sometimes known as Deborah's Hole camp, has semicircular ramparts that cut off an area of six thousand one hundred square metres or approximately one a half acres. Inside the ramparts nothing of an Iron Age date is visible, however, in 1938 the site was excavated by Audrey Williams and the remains of two round houses were found (Whittle 1992: 51-2). Finds recovered indicate a mixed economy was practiced at the site and including potboilers, shells, bones of sheep/goats and oxen. Across the entrance were traces of three postholes suggesting this site was sealed by double gates (Williams 1939: 213-4). Pottery sherds were recovered from a roundhouse on the north side of the site and represent at least seven vessels; all are handmade. The material varies in colour from pale buff to grey-black and has a generally smooth burnished surface.

The pottery from this site also shows affinities with pottery recovered from Glastonbury (Bullied and Gray 1911-17) and is dated to the 1st century BC (Williams 1939: 218).

Portskewett School - SO 4983 8833

Trial excavations carried out on the proposed school site at Portskewett revealed substantial evidence of Iron Age occupation. Items recovered include Iron Age pottery of calcite-tempered ware similar in form to that recovered from nearby Sudbrook (Nash-Williams 1939). The majority of the sherds appear to be the remnants of jars or bowls but also include the remains of a large vessel and a fragment of a handle. Other sherds are present but are different in form and are waiting for further diagnosis. A number of large clay fragments were recovered reminiscent of very coarse pottery or 'VCP' which was first recognised from Sutton Walls and Croft Ambrey, thought to be small stoves as described by Stanford (1974:

Pottery sherds, hammer stone, mace head, slingstones and potboilers. S.W.S: A952. 42.1 through 19 Slingstones from large heap. S.W.S: AX57

Objects of unknown character. S.W.S: A965.22

Mixture of pottery, conglomerate, daub fragments and slingstones. S.W.S: A938.42.1/2.

Material culture

The material culture recovered from The Knave Promontory Fort is housed at Swansea Museum.

Pottery sherds, hammer stone, mace head, slingstones and potboilers. S.W.S: A952. 42.1 through 19.

Slingstones from large heap. S.W.S: AX57

Objects of unknown character. S.W.S: A965.22

Mixture of pottery, conglomerate, daub fragments and slingstones.S.W.S:A938.42

210-14). More recently vessels of this type have been associated with the salt industry at Droitwich (Clark et al 1999: 84-5). One La Tène 1 brooch was found in a fixed stratigraphical context and is dated to between 400 BC and 250 BC. This is a one piece brooch with a large six-coiled spring and made of a copper alloy; a comparable brooch from Wales was found at Merthyr Mawr Warren (Savory 1976: 25, 67 figure 35.15; Morris 1985, 1994). The second brooch is a copper alloy pennanular brooch with the pin missing (Clark et al 1999: 84-5). This example corresponds with Fowler 's Type A1 classification that she dates to approximately 300 BC and 100 BC (Fowler 1960).

Sudbrook – ST 505 873

Excavations were carried out at the coastal hillfort at Sudbrook during 1934 and 1935 by Nash-Williams. The hillfort as seen today has been reduced in size by coastal erosion. The site is enclosed by a massive, well preserved bank with two, possibly three smaller banks on the north-west side but no outer bank is visible on the north-east side (Nash-Williams 1939) The material culture recovered indicates occupation of this site from the mid-2nd century BC to the early part of the 2nd century AD. The material culture also indicates that the Roman army occupied this site sometime around 50 AD, perhaps to guard the ferry crossing between Portskewett and Aust (Nash-Williams 1939; Whittle 1992: 49).

Material culture

The material culture recovered from Sudbrook is housed at the National Museum and Gallery of Wales, Cardiff.

Adornment

Iron tweezers coated in bronze. N.M.W: 36.438.19. See figure 86.

Copper alloy La Téne III brooch. N.M.W: 35.389.4. See figure 87.

Copper alloy La Téne III brooch. N.M.W: 35.438.14.

Part of a bow brooch and open catch plate. N.M.W: unknown.

Ten-coiled spring bronze brooch with five springs on each side. N.M.W: unknown. See figure 88.

Ten-coiled spring brooch with six springs on the one side and four on the other. N.M.W: unknown. See figure 89.

Ten-coiled spring bronze brooch with five springs on each side. N.M.W: unknown. See figure 90.

Ten-coiled spring brooch with six springs on the one side and four on the other. N.M.W: unknown. See figure 91.

Fragment of a bronze knobbed headed pin. See figure 92. N.M.W: unknown.

Fragment of a bronze pin, bent. N.M.W: unknown.

Fragmentary coiled spring and pin of a bronze brooch. N.M.W: unknown.

Ten-coiled spring bronze brooch with five springs on each side. N.M.W: unknown. Bronze brooch. N.M.W: unknown.

Ten-coiled spring bronze brooch with five springs on each side. N.M.W: unknown.

Glass bead. N.M.W: unknown.

Glass bead. N.M.W: unknown.

Animal Bones

The skeletal remains of a number of animals were recovered and due to the very poor condition of the remains the size and amount of animal represented could not be determined. Species represented include oxen, sheep/goat, pig, horse, red deer, badger, otter and rabbit (Cowley in Nash-Williams 1939: 78-9). N.M.W: unknown.

Coins

Tiberius (*c.* AD 12). *Reverse*: [ROM ET AVG]. Altar. Probably from the Lugdunum mint, this coin was in a worn condition. N.M.W: unknown.

Claudius (*c.* AD 41-54). *Reverse S.C*: Image of Minerva fighting; this coin is an imitation and was in a worn condition. N.M.W: unknown.

Vespasian (AD 71). *Reverse:* Uncertain. Probably of the Lugdunum mint, this example is in a poor condition. (Mattingly in Nash-Williams 1939: 77). N.M.W: unknown.

Domestic Production

Quern stone. N.M.W: 34.479.

Spindle whorl made of lead. N.M.W: unknown

Spindle whorl made of sandstone. N.M.W: unknown.

Spindle whorl made from a fragment of pottery. N.M.W: unknown.

Horse

Bronze mounting with rivets. N.M.W: unknown.

Mounting of cast bronze with loop and eyelet holes. See figure 93. N.M.W: unknown.

Pottery

A variety of pottery. N.M.W: 36.438.1 through to N.M.W: 36.438.23.

Pottery fragments. N.M.W: 99.36.H.2.

Pottery rim sherds. N.M.W: 77.8.

Production

Rough coiled strip of lead. N.M.W: unknown.

Small fragment of crucible made of baked clay that has traces of bronze fused to it. N.M.W: unknown.

Fifteen iron nails. N.M.W: unknown.

Iron mount. N.M.W: unknown.

Iron ring. N.M.W: unknown.

Iron mounting. N.M.W: unknown.

Iron nail. N.M.W: unknown.

Iron plate with keyhole piercing. N.M.W: unknown.

Iron plate/strip. N.M.W: unknown.

Iron shank or bar. N.M.W: unknown.

Tools

Knife tang with curved blade. N.M.W: 35.389.

Fragmentary knife. N.M.W: unknown.

Fragmentary knife. N.M.W: unknown.

Iron awl. N.M.W: unknown.

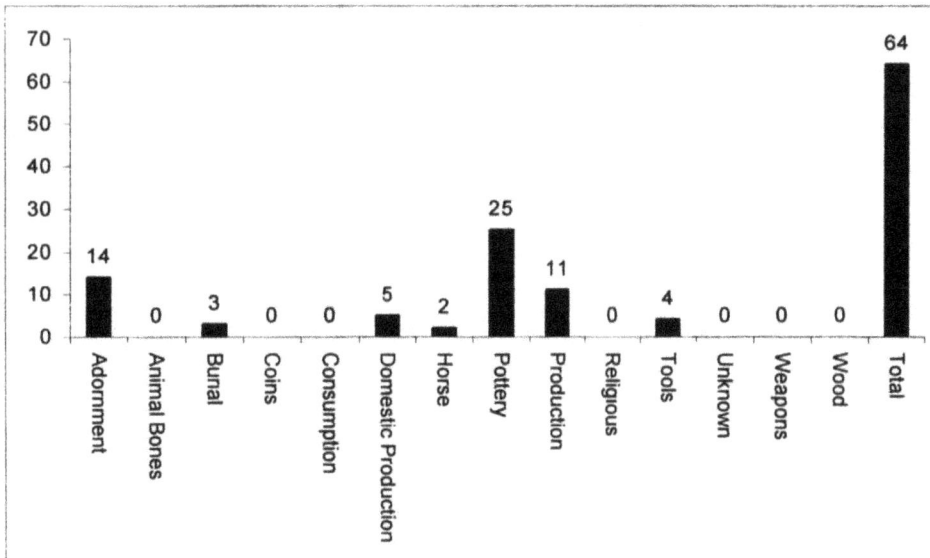

Table 13. Ratio of material culture from Sudbrook excavation.

Twyn y Gaer – SO 294 219

Excavation by a small team of workers drawn from the Abergavenny Archaeological Group began at this site in the mid-sixties. Although excavation finished in the mid-seventies, the work supervised by Probert (1976) remains unpublished. The hillfort of Twyn y Gaer encloses an area of 1.8 hectares and is partly bivallate. Excavations revealed that the site had a complex life, this coupled with the multitude of artefacts found here, highlights the importance of publishing the findings of this site. The interim report by Probert (1976) only hints at the potential at Twyn y Gaer for archaeological research. A large variety of material culture was recovered from this site including pieces that are chronologically diagnostic. Included in this assemblage are seventeen brooches of La Téne I and II representing one of the most important brooch assemblages in Britain.

Material culture

The material culture recovered from Twyn y Gaer is housed at The National Museum and Gallery, Cardiff.

Adornment

There is limited information available for the brooches from Twyn y Gaer. The excavation by Probert (1976) was conducted mainly upon the East and West Gates, where rubbish accumulated in the angles of the inturned rampart. Iron La Tène straight rod and involuted brooches were found here and show marked similarities to those at Croft Ambrey (Stanford 1974). Attempts have been made to determine the evolution of the brooches by the form of the foot in relation to the bow, but the stratigraphical occurrence of the Twyn y Gaer brooches suggests that the heads of the brooches may provide a more useful line of enquiry. The early examples from Twyn y Gaer have functional springs, but in later deposits, a change occurs towards a hinged type employing a spindle that still has the appearance of a spring. In a later example, no springs are present but a pierced ring-hinge is used (Probert 1976: 115).

Possible La Tène I brooch. N.M.W: 90.109.H.7.

La Téne II brooch (Arras culture) N.M.W: 90.109.H.8

Brooch pin. N.M.W: 90.109.H.9.

Iron brooch. N.M.W: 90.109.H.10.

Brooch pin. N.M.W: 90.109.H.12.

Iron brooch. N.M.W: 90.109.H.14.

Iron brooch. N.M.W: 90.109.H.15.

Iron involuted brooch. N.M.W: 90.109.H.35.

Possible involuted brooch. N.M.W: 90.110.H.6.

Involuted brooch. N.M.W: 90.110.H.7.

Brooch spring. N.M.W: 90.110.H.9.

Involuted brooch. N.M.W: 90.110.H.11.

Brooch pin. N.M.W: 90.110.H.12.

Involuted brooch. N.M.W: 90.110.H.13.

Iron brooch. N.M.W: 90.110.H.20.

Possible brooch pin. N.M.W: 90.111.H.7.

Possible involuted brooch. N.M.W: 90.119.H.6.

Nine Iron Age glass bead. N.M.W: 90.109.H.

Fragment of iron bracelet. N.M.W: 90.109.H.33.

Domestic Production

Latch lifter. N.M.W: 90.109.H.28.

Potboiler. N.M.W: unknown.

Bolt. N.M.W: 90.109.H.

Horse

This item could be a belt hook fitting for use with horses or humans. N.M.W: 90.110.H.2.

Pottery

Conjoining sherds of small to medium size vessels. N.M.W: 90.109.H.19.

Very coarse pottery thought to be fragments of salt conveyors. N.M.W: 90.109.H.2.

Production

Copper alloy well worked, possible prestigious item. N.M.W: 90.109.H.6.

Iron stud. N.M.W: 90.109.H.16.

Piece of iron shaped like the sole of a shoe. N.M.W: 90.109.H.22.

Fragment of iron plate sheet. N.M.W: 90.109.H.23.

Bar with a loop attached made from a substantial amount of iron. N.M.W: 90.109.H.29.

Oval ring. N.M.W: 90.109.H.32.

Iron ring. N.M.W: 90.110.H.15.

Socket or binding pieces with pin. N.M.W: 90.110.H.17.

Iron staple. N.M.W: 90.111.H.6.

Tools

Knife blade. N.M.W: 90.109.H.20.

Iron file with markings. N.M.W: 90.109.H.30.

Stripping tool. H.M.W: 90.109.H.31.

Knife blade. N.M.W: 90.109.H.34.

Chisel. N.M.W: 90.110.H.5.

Possible knife blade. N.M.W: 90.110.H.10.

Cleat. N.M.W: 90.110.H.14.

Handle. N.M.W: 90.111.H.2.

Knife. N.M.W: 90.111.H.4.

Knife blade. N.M.W: 90.111.H.8.

Possible chisel. N.M.W: 90.111.H.9.

Unknown

Some sort of fitting, type unknown. N.M.W: 90.111.H.1.

Weapons

Sword. N.M.W: unknown.

Sword hilt guard. N.M.W: 90.109.H.21.

Spear ferrel butt. N.M.W: 90.110.H.4.

Sling stones. N.M.W: unknown.

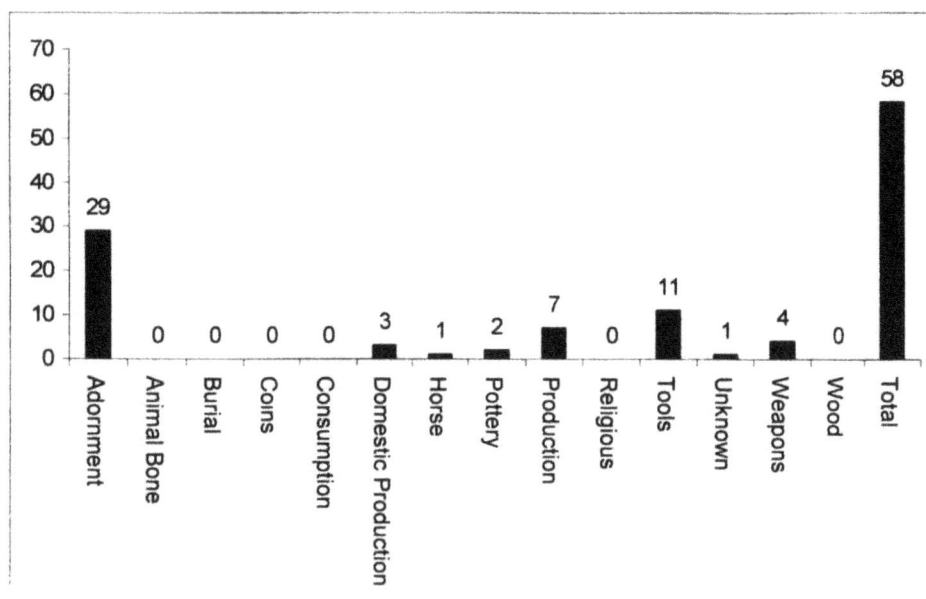

Table 14. Ratio of materials recovered from Twyn y Gaer excavations.

Whitton, South Glamorgan – ST 081 713

Excavation began in 1965 at the Iron Age and Roman farm at Whitton and continued until 1970. The work was conducted by M.G. Jarrett and the Department of Archaeology, University College, Cardiff. The results of the excavation revealed that the earliest artefacts recorded, apart from a handful of flints, include a glass bead which might be dated as early as the 3rd century BC and other beads that may be dated to the 2nd or 1st centuries BC (Jarrett and Wrathmell 1981: 4). There is no evidence to suggest that occupation of the site began as early as this and no evidence of clearly stratified Iron Age levels, except for the lowest level in the entrance, below the first laid surface. None of the Iron Age objects recovered would be out of place in the 1st century AD, although some may have been introduced earlier (Jarrett and Wrathmell 1981: 5). The small amount of Iron Age material recovered does not suggest occupation during the Early Iron Age at Whitton, a date of c. AD 30 or later has been suggested for the beginning of occupation here.

Material culture

Brooch made of thin bronze metal with a cylindrical cover for the hinged pin, curved forward to the front of the brooch. A Langdon Down derivative (Webster 1988: 165; 166 fig 1). See figure 94.

T-shaped brooch made of bronze with cylindrical crossbar, housing the pivot of the hinged pin. The bow is of a D-shaped cross-section at the head and tapers to a knife-edge foot that is bent out of shape. This example has been dated to the early or mid 1st century AD (Webster 1988: 165; 166 fig 2). See figure 95.

Hod Hill La Téne III brooch made of bronze. The upper part of bow tapers slightly and is ornamented with four longitudinal knurled ridges with three broad intervening flutings with traces of silvering. This example has been dated to the early or mid 1st century AD (Webster 1981: 165; 166 fig 3). See figure 96.

45

Hod Hill derivative brooch made of bronze with a hinged pin on an iron pivot. The bow is slightly curved and tapers towards the foot and is decorated with two grooves running longitudinally down the centre. One groove is further decorated by a dot ornament. This example has been dated to the early or mid 1st century AD (Webster 1988: 165; 166 fig 4). See figure 97.

The following six brooches belong to Hull's Light Polden category (see Winchester 1949-60 fig. 24, no 1; Richborough V, 75-6). Brooches of this type occur in some numbers in South Wales in the first century AD. They are categorised by a bronze flap that projects from the side-wings concealing a large spring. Dated examples in the area are hard to find but the example from Sudbrook

(Nash-Williams 1939: 74-5) lies within the period AD 50-75 (Webster 1988: 167).

Brooch one has a slight ovoid curve and is in square cross-section, the bow is narrow and tapers (Webster 1988: 166, fig. 5). See figure 98.

Brooch two has broad and almost flat side-wings, the bow tapers and is badly bent (Webster 1988: 168, fig. 6). See figure 99.

Brooch three has broad almost flat side-wings and the plain bow tapers to a knife- edge (Webster 1988: 168, fig. 7). See figure 100.

Brooch four is a spring and pin that probably belonged to a similar type to the above entry (Webster 1988: 168, fig 7a). See figure 101.

Brooch five is in a very poor condition, each of the side wings has hatched bands and the bow is bent out of shape (Webster 1988: 168, fig 8). See figure 102.

Brooch six has side wings that are ornamented and the bow is very narrow and tapers to a knife-edge foot (Webster 1988: 168, fig 9). See figure 103.

Iron pennanular brooch, the ring has a sub-rectangular section and small rectangular terminals. Iron pennanular brooches are relatively rare but examples have been recorded from Verulamium (Manning 1972: 180 fig 66 and 57). This example is of Fowler's Type A1 (Fowler 1960: 149); Webster et al 1981: 189 fig 25; 193 item 25). N.M.W: W66LX.225. See figure 104.

Pennanular brooch, the ring is circular in cross section with the terminals at right angles to the plane of the ring and is in a poor condition. This example belongs to Fowler type D, 1st century BC to 3rd century AD (Fowler 1960: 151 fig. 1, 152 and 176; Webster et al 1988: 176 fig 29; 177). See figure 105.

Pennanular brooch, twisted out of shape, belongs to Fowlers Group D1or D4; in poor condition. Terminals at right angles to the plane of the ring. Fowler type D, 1st century BC to 3rd century AD or 1st to 3rd century AD (Fowler 1960: 151 fig. 1, 152 and 176; Webster et al 1981: 176 fig. 30, 177). See figure 106.

Pennanular brooch with circular cross section belongs to Fowlers Group D1 and D2, dated to either 1st to 3rd c AD or 1st to 4th century AD (Fowler 1960: 151 fig. 1, 152 and 176; Webster et al 1988: 176 fig 31; 177). See figure 107.

Lowest part of the bow of a bronze brooch with an elaborate openwork catch-plate. The bow is decorated with a central beaded rib. The foot is damaged and without the upper part of the brooch and spring, identification is difficult but an early to mid 1st century AD date is not unreasonable (Webster et al 1988: 187 fi6 fig 105; 188).

Shale bracelet fragments; four fragments in all but one-piece remains unpublished; all are housed together at the National Museum and Gallery of Wales, Cardiff. (Lawson 1988: 225-6 fig. 86). N.M.W: W66LX. 225.

Fragment of opaque yellow bead with translucent brown horns applied to the outside surface and bound with fine opaque yellow trails. Glass beads. (Price 1988: 160). N.M.W: W66LX.160.
Glass bead. N.M.W: 77.40.H.8.

Bridle bit links. (Manning and Scott 1988: 189, fig. 20; 192).
N.M.W: W66LX.20.

Bridle bit links. (Manning and Scott 1988: 189, fig. 21; 192). N.M.W: W66LX.21.

Metal cross section for holding a cauldron or firedog (Manning and Scott 1988: 195 fig 47; 196). N.M.W: W66LX.47.

Chisel set (Manning 1988: 189; 191 fig. 8). N.M.W: W66LX.5.

Mason's pick made of iron with a long sub-rectangular eye. This piece is characteristic of Iron Age tools (Manning and Scott 1988: 189 fig. 10; 191). See figure 108. N.M.W: W66LX.10.

Iron ingot. N.M.W: 77.40.H.3.

Discussion and Conclusion

Of the many Iron Age sites that are recorded in Wales, only a small percentage have been excavated. Although excavation has been a rare occurrence, when it has been undertaken material culture is nearly always recovered.

Admittedly, the amounts are not large but what is recovered is usually of a very high quality and often chronologically diagnostic. The items outlined in the previous chapters illustrate the diverse nature of material culture accessible for study in south-east Wales. The sites included in this chapter demonstrate that during the Iron Age the inhabitants of this region utilized a diverse range of locations and exploited a variety of differing landscapes.

The majority of the sites included in this book were excavated decades ago without the benefit of modern day excavation techniques. The need for re-evaluation and the application of scientific analysis with the aim of establishing firm dates where possible is a priority if we are to have a better understanding of occupation patterns in this region and in Wales as a whole during the Iron Age. The artefacts discussed in this chapter have been recovered from various locations including wetland areas such as those investigated on the Gwent Levels. An assortment of material has been recovered from these sites including a number of organic materials. Finds of organic materials are rare and are always an important factor in providing a more complete picture of life in the past.

Analysis of the occupation of caves in this region is frequently forgotten, yet evidence from a number of caves indicates that sites where being occupied during the Iron Age. A re-evaluation of caves and their uses is needed in order to establish the nature of the relationship between these sites and settlements and others that were in close proximity to them. The main concentration of archaeological research in past decades has been concentrated either on coastal or inland hillforts. Whilst hilltop occupation was obviously an important feature of the Iron Age, focus needs to be shifted from single site analysis to a more homogenous approach in order to establish what relationships existed, if any, between all Iron Age sites.

o By re-evaluating and analysing the material culture recovered from excavations there is the potential to:

o Aid in establishing reliable dates for individual sites

o Identify processes of change in the material culture record by investigating inclusions and exclusions of artefacts groups.

o Enable archaeologists to establish what contacts the people of this region had with other areas, this can be achieved through the application of scientific analysis and chronological diagnosis to many of the artefacts

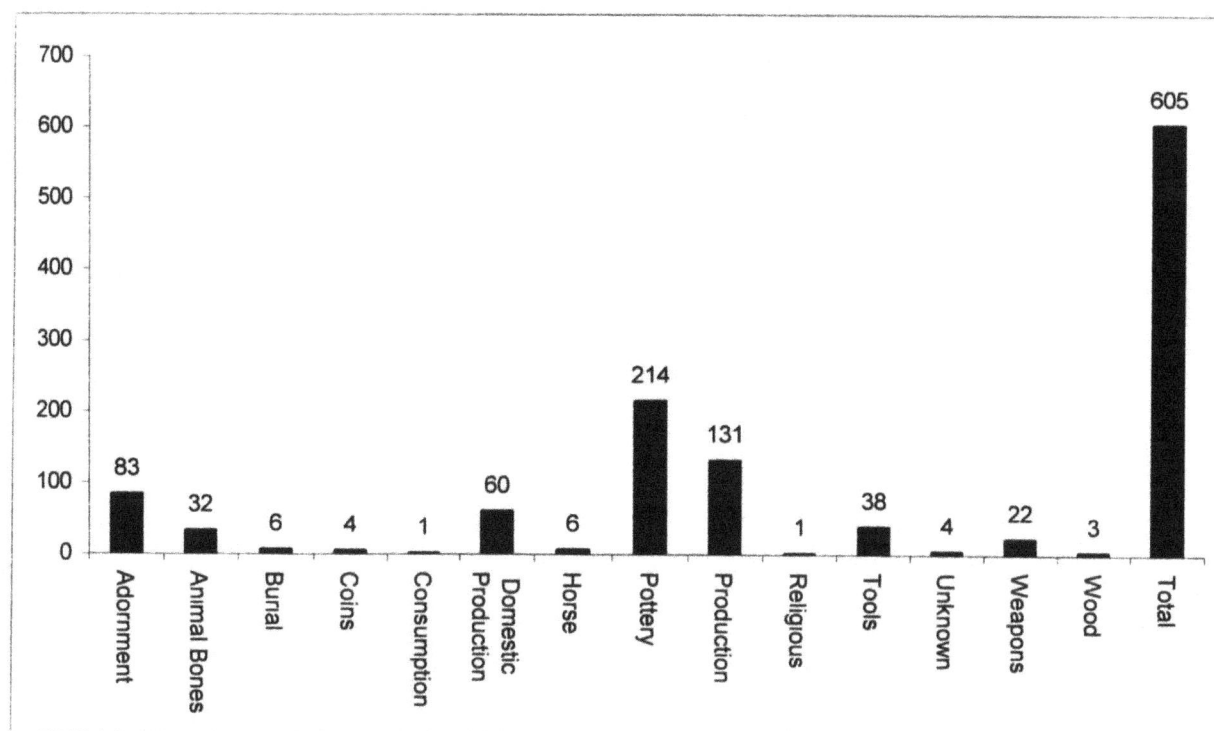

Table 15. Total ratios of the material culture recorded.

Table 15 shows that a wide range of artefacts has been recorded with a higher ratio of pottery fragments in comparison to the others. Objects used in both domestic and manufacturing production processes are also visible as are tools, which is not surprising considering they would have been used in both domestic and manufacturing situations. Whilst a number of fragmented pottery sherd have been recovered there is a lack of objects concerned with the consumption of food and drink, possibly reflecting that little work has been conducted upon the forms of the vessels collected from the study area. The lack of high status feasting vessels could also indicate that the sites included were not residences of an elite but of everyday Iron Age individual that tended the land and exploited the resources that were at hand.

There are a large amount of objects listed under adornment and the majority of those are complete or fragmentary brooches. Many of these examples are chronologically diagnostic, whilst a number have no stratigraphical contexts. Contact and exchange patterns between people of different regions can be traced through the examination of the stylistic tendencies and chronologies of artefact typologies. Clearly, more excavations of Iron Age sites as well as the re-evaluation of the material culture from past excavations would expand archaeologist's understanding of the interaction of these sites in the past.

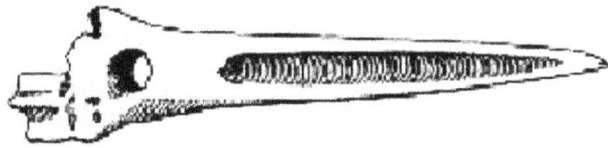

68

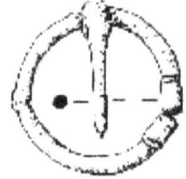

69

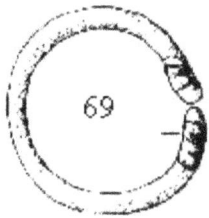

70

71

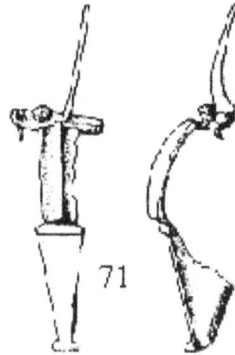

72

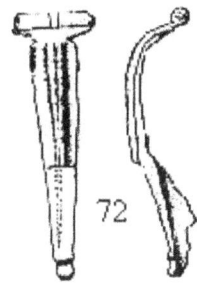

73

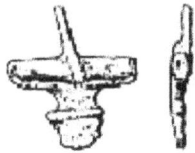

75

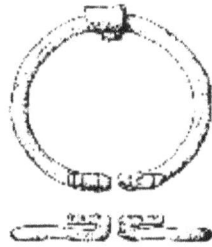

76

77

78

79

80

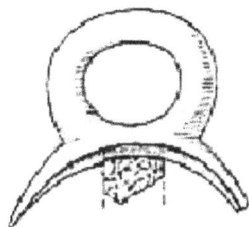

Figure 81. Human remains from Llanmelin.

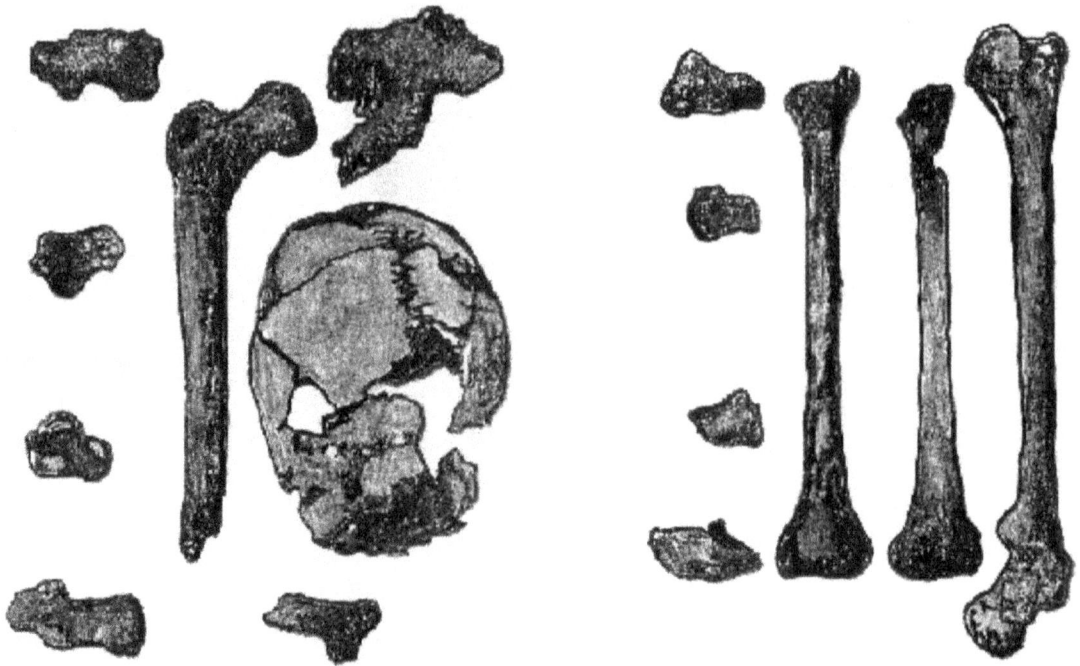

Figure 82. La Téne brooch from Lodge Hill

Figure 83. Two ring headed pins from Merthyr Mawr

Lodge Hill 7000
scale 2:1

Figure 85. Spiral bronze ring from Mynydd Bychan

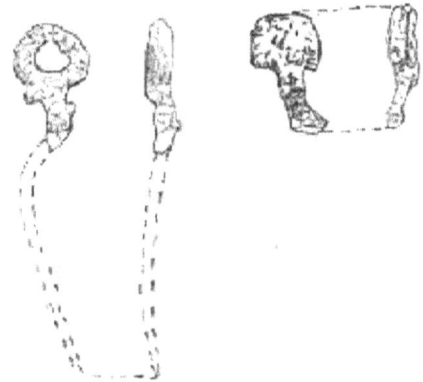

Figure 84. La Téne I brooch from Merthyr Mawr

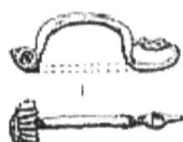

Figure87. La Tene III brooch from Sudbrook

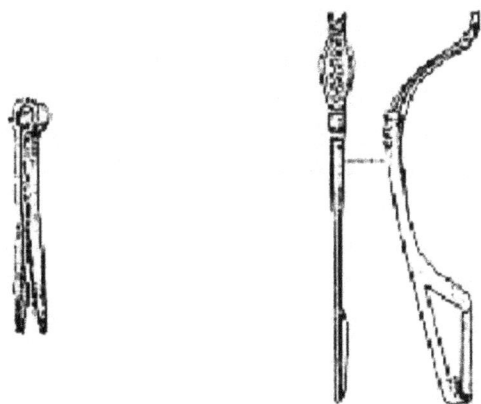

Figure 88. Brooch from Sudbrook

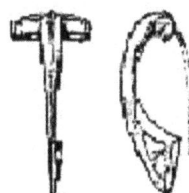

Figure 89. Brooch from Sudbrook

Figure 90. Brooch from Sudbrook

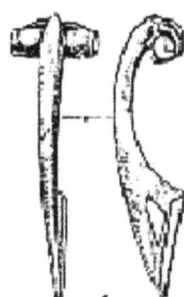

Figure 91. Brooch from Sudbrook

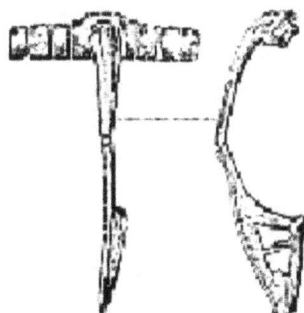

Figure 92. Bronze headed pin Sudbrook

Figure 94. Brooch from Whitton

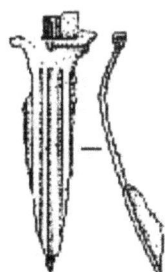

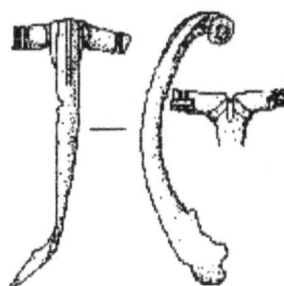

Figure 96. Brooch from Whitton

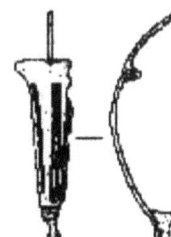

Figure 98. Brooch from Whitton

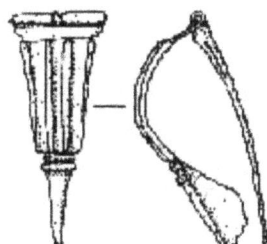

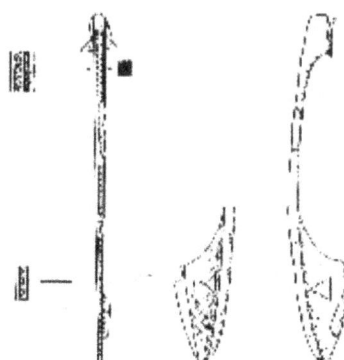

Figure 99. Brooch from Whitton

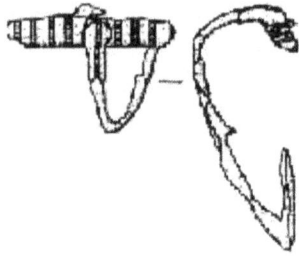

Figure 100. Brooch from Whitton

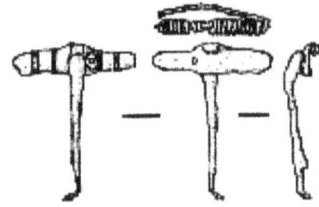

Figure 101 Brooch from Whitton

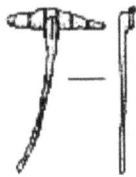

Figure 103. Brooch from Whitton

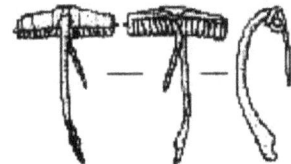

Figure 102. Brooch from Whitton

Figure 104. Pennanular brooch from Whitton

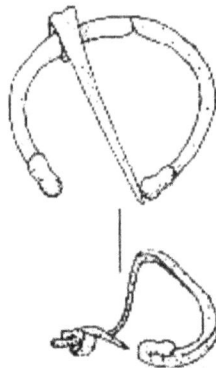

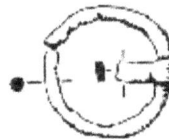

Figure 105. Pennanular brooch from Whitton

Figure 106. Pennanular brooch from Whitton

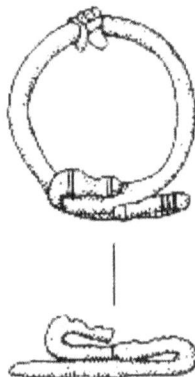

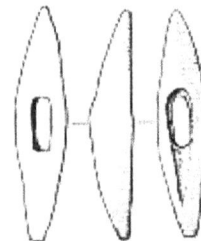

Figure 107. Pennanular brooch from Whitton

Figure 108. Masons pick from Whitton

52

Chapter 7

Conclusion and Discussion

In conclusion, as the title of this paper states, clearly, there are artefacts available from the Iron Age in Wales. From the small area covered in this paper alone there is plenty that has been recovered for recording and examination. As stated earlier there is no comprehensive listing of what has been found, which has caused confusion or the misapprehension that there is a dearth of Iron Age material culture in Wales and what is there, is not of a high enough quality to be useful in informing archaeologists's understanding of the Iron Age in Wales. The purpose of compiling the information regarding artefacts in south-east Wales was to show that through the collection and collation of disparate and fragmentary information just how much material culture is available in a relatively small area and how much potential there is in this information for further research. This paper was intended as an empirical study rather than a theoretical debate concerning the material presented. Although, theoretical discussion is very important and does facilitate our understanding of the past, the compiling of corpuses of information is equally important and provides the framework upon which theory is structured.

As illustrated in the previous chapters, much can be learned from the material culture that is discussed in this paper. In Chapter 4, the presentation of chance finds illustrates that the majority of these, whilst limited in what information they can supply, are varied in style and purpose. The diverse and obscure nature of many of the objects discussed in this chapter raises a number of questions that need to be addressed by future research, such as how did the objects end up in their final resting place, and how can the distribution of such an obscure set of objects inform our understanding of this region during the Iron Age. Many of the pieces found are important, as they can be chronologically diagnostic providing a fuller picture of Iron Age life.

The hoards discussed in Chapter 5 highlight another area of study that is important to understanding what was occurring at this time. Hoards seem to occur more at times of stress, a pattern that is particularly evident during the Roman invasion in the Later Iron Age. Hoards in the earlier phases of the Iron Age seemed to have had more of a ritual purpose, whereas hoards from the Late Iron Age tend to be Founder's hoards which were buried for later retrieval. Objects in the later hoards are of a particularly high standard of craftsmanship. This may be due to increased contacts with other people from different regions of the Britain and Europe. Most of these hoards include objects that have parallels in other parts of Britain and even Europe, supporting the suggestion of wide exchange contacts. Until further research is done on chronologies and typologies of the artefacts included in this chapter, verification of their original provenance is debatable. Comparison between hoards found in other parts of Wales, the rest of the Britain and Europe would be a useful tool for discovering patterns of behaviour, exchange and contact and the temporal placement of them during the British Iron Age.

After beginning my research, I discovered that there were more excavated sites in south-east Wales than I first believed, and for this reason, I have not been able to include all the excavated sites in this paper. However, the information compiled from the sites that I have discussed in Chapter 5 is very useful as an example of a selection of what has been recovered and what is available for study. The excavation of sites that have evidence of occupation indicates that there was not the dense population occurring here that is evident in Iron Age sites in southern England and Europe. It does confirm, however, that settlement was occurring but sites like hillforts were utilized differently and on a smaller scale. The evidence of the excavation points to the small-scale production, in both the domestic and the industrial sense. This is evident through the discovery of crucibles and other production components referred to in the previous chapter. Another aspect of settlement that becomes apparent from excavation is the diverse type of locations being occupied and exploited in this region at this time. Examples of the variability in occupation include the cave sites on the Gower peninsula, the lowland wetland sites at Goldcliff as well as inland and coastal hilltop occupation in Gwent and Glamorgan.

Considering the small percentage of Iron Age sites that have been excavated in the two regions discussed in this paper and coupled with those artefacts recovered as chance finds and in hoards, the amount of material from this region, whilst not on the same scale as that found on sites in southern England, is still considerable and is of a high quality. If this is true of the small area of Wales covered in this investigation, the amount of material in the rest of Wales is undoubtedly more robust than previously believed. If the same amount of time, money and attention were focused on other sites in Wales as it has been in other parts of Britain, it is quite likely that the picture of Iron Age Wales would change significantly. This is true of artefact studies as well.

	Repository	Place of find	Category	Assec No	Artefact Type	Material
1	Repository	Place of find	Category	Assec No	Artefact Type	Material
2	NMW	All-wern	chance find	98.19H	La Tene strap union (stage five La Tene)	strap
3	NMW	Bacon Hole Cave	Excavation	42.62/1	IA pottery sherds	pottery
4	NMW	Bigliss	Excavation	82.68H/2	bone point	bone
5	NMW	Bigliss	Excavation	82.68H/2	twisted copper alloy band fragment	bronze
6	NMW	Bigliss	Excavation	82.68H/2	pennanular brooch	brooch
7	NMW	Bigliss	Excavation	82.68H/2	pennanular brooch poor condition	brooch
8	NMW	Bigliss	Excavation	82.68H/2	casket ornament	caskett ornament
9	NMW	Black Pill	chance find	98.14H	IA copper alloy terret	terret
10	NMW	Broughton Burrows	chance find	78.41H/6	IA body sherd (uncertain)	pottery
11	NMW	Broughton Burrows	chance find	78.41H/8	IA rim sherd	pottery
12	NMW	Burrows Well	chance find	53.459/11	EIA pottery	pottery
13	NMW	Burry Holms Island	Excavation	98.36H/125	IA glass bead	bead
14	NMW	Burry Holms Island	Excavation	98.36H/126	IA pottery sherd	pottery
15	NMW	Burry Holms Island	Excavation	98.36H/71	IA potsherds	pottery
16	NMW	Burry Holms Island	Excavation	98.36H/72	IA potsherds	pottery
17	NMW	Burry Holms Island	Excavation	99.43H/279	IA glass bead	bead
18	NMW	Burry Holms Island	Excavation	99.43H/287	IA potsherds	pottery
19	NMW	Caerleon	chance find	31.78	LIA sword hilt LIA.	sword
20	NMW	Caerleon	chance find	31.78/116	EIA copper alloy leech pin	bronze
21	PA	Caerwent area - outside Roman wall	chance find	1999, 63 and 99.96.1	possible torc fragment - knobbed piece	torc
22	NPT	Caerwent Quarry	chance find	84.05.5	5: central body sherd; 6: rim sherd; 7: section with double beaded rim	pottery
23	NMW	Castle Ditches/Llancarfan	Excavation	84.33H/2	bronze terret/harness ring	terret
24	NMW	Castle Ditches/Llancarfan	Excavation	84.33H/3	bronze nail cleaner with forked end	nail cleaner
25	NPT	Chapel Tump	Excavation	85.218	rim fragment, beaded LIA	pottery
26	NPT	Chapel Tump	Excavation	88.91	hurdle trackway c14 dated to IA, pegs, rods and sails, also brushwood and leaves.	wood
27	NMW	Chepstow	chance find	35.304	harness mount in S-scroll with knobbed terminals and corresponding knob.	harness
28	NPT	Chepstow area	chance find	89.233	grotesque in form	mount
29	NMW	Coed y Cymdda	Excavation	91.2H/100	utilised stone	stone
30	NMW	Coed y Cymdda	Excavation	91.2H/101	utilised stone	stone
31	NMW	Coed y Cymdda	Excavation	91.2H/102	utilised stone	stone
32	NMW	Coed y Cymdda	Excavation	91.2H/103	utilised stone	stone
33	NMW	Coed y Cymdda	Excavation	91.2H/104	utilised stone	stone
34	NMW	Coed y Cymdda	Excavation	91.2H/105	utilised stone	stone
35	NMW	Coed y Cymdda	Excavation	91.2H/106	sample of quartz	quartz
36	NMW	Coed y Cymdda	Excavation	91.2H/107	samples of hearmatite	sample
37	NMW	Coed y Cymdda	Excavation	91.2H/108	samples of hearmatite	sample
38	NMW	Coed y Cymdda	Excavation	91.2H/109	samples of hearmatite	sample
39	NMW	Coed y Cymdda	Excavation	91.2H/110	samples of hearmatite	sample
40	NMW	Coed y Cymdda	Excavation	91.2H/111	samples of hearmatite	sample

	A	B	C	D	E	G
41	NMW	Coed y Cymdda	Excavation	91.2H/112	samples of heamatite	sample
42	NMW	Coed y Cymdda	Excavation	91.2H/113	samples of heamatite	sample
43	NMW	Coed y Cymdda	Excavation	91.2H/114	samples of heamatite	sample
44	NMW	Coed y Cymdda	Excavation	91.2H/115	samples of heamatite	sample
45	NMW	Coed y Cymdda	Excavation	91.2H/116	samples of heamatite	sample
46	NMW	Coed y Cymdda	Excavation	91.2H/117	samples of heamatite	sample
47	NMW	Coed y Cymdda	Excavation	91.2H/118	samples of heamatite	sample
48	NMW	Coed y Cymdda	Excavation	91.2H/119	samples of heamatite	sample
49	NMW	Coed y Cymdda	Excavation	91.2H/120	samples of heamatite	sample
50	NMW	Coed y Cymdda	Excavation	91.2H/121	samples of iron ore	sample
51	NMW	Coed y Cymdda	Excavation	91.2H/122	samples of iron ore	sample
52	NMW	Coed y Cymdda	Excavation	91.2H/123	samples of heamatite	sample
53	NMW	Coed y Cymdda	Excavation	91.2H/61	IA potsherds	pottery
54	NMW	Coed y Cymdda	Excavation	91.2H/62	EIA potsherd	pottery
55	NMW	Coed y Cymdda	Excavation	91.2H/66	BA/IA whetstone	stone
56	NMW	Coed y Cymdda	Excavation	91.2H/67	BA/IA whetstone	stone
57	NMW	Coed y Cymdda	Excavation	91.2H/68	BA/IA whetstone	stone
58	NMW	Coed y Cymdda	Excavation	91.2H/69	BA/IA whetstone	stone
59	NMW	Coed y Cymdda	Excavation	91.2H/70	BA/IA whetstone	stone
60	NMW	Coed y Cymdda	Excavation	91.2H/71	BA/IA whetstone	stone
61	NMW	Coed y Cymdda	Excavation	91.2H/72	BA/IA whetstone	stone
62	NMW	Coed y Cymdda	Excavation	91.2H/73	BA/IA whetstone	stone
63	NMW	Coed y Cymdda	Excavation	91.2H/75	IA pot boiler	stone
64	NMW	Coed y Cymdda	Excavation	91.2H/76	IA pot boiler	stone
65	NMW	Coed y Cymdda	Excavation	91.2H/77	sample of heamatite	sample
66	NMW	Coed y Cymdda	Excavation	91.2H/78	IA hearth stone	hearth
67	NMW	Coed y Cymdda	Excavation	91.2H/79	sample of meta rhyolite	sample
68	NMW	Coed y Cymdda	Excavation	91.2H/80	IA pot boilers	stone
69	NMW	Coed y Cymdda	Excavation	91.2H/81	IA pot boilers	stone
70	NMW	Coed y Cymdda	Excavation	91.2H/82	IA pot boilers	stone
71	NMW	Coed y Cymdda	Excavation	91.2H/83	IA pot boilers	stone
72	NMW	Coed y Cymdda	Excavation	91.2H/84	IA pot boilers	stone
73	NMW	Coed y Cymdda	Excavation	91.2H/85	IA pot boilers	stone
74	NMW	Coed y Cymdda	Excavation	91.2H/86	IA pot boilers	stone
75	NMW	Coed y Cymdda	Excavation	91.2H/87	IA pot boilers	stone
76	NMW	Coed y Cymdda	Excavation	91.2H/88	IA pot boilers	stone
77	NMW	Coed y Cymdda	Excavation	91.2H/89	IA sling shot	stone
78	NMW	Coed y Cymdda	Excavation	91.2H/90	IA sling shot	stone
79	NMW	Coed y Cymdda	Excavation	91.2H/91	IA sling shot	stone
80	NMW	Coed y Cymdda	Excavation	91.2H/92	IA rotary quern	quern

	A	B	C	D	E	G
81	NMW	Coed y Cymdda	Excavation	91.2H/93	utilised stone	stone
82	NMW	Coed y Cymdda	Excavation	91.2H/94	utilised stone	stone
83	NMW	Coed y Cymdda	Excavation	91.2H/95	utilised stone	stone
84	NMW	Coed y Cymdda	Excavation	91.2H/96	utilised stone	stone
85	NMW	Coed y Cymdda	Excavation	91.2H/97	utilised stone	stone
86	NMW	Coed y Cymdda	Excavation	91.2H/98	utilised stone	stone
87	NMW	Coed y Cymdda	Excavation	91.2H/99	utilised stone	stone
88	NMW	Colcot	chance find	62.92/1	EIA pottery	pottery
89	PA	Cowbridge	chance find	2001.45.1	strap union	strap
90	NMW	Culver Hole Cave	chance find	25.221/5	IA glass bead	bead
91	NMW	Darren Fort	chance find	87.44H/4	lead ore fragment	lead
92	SWS	Knave Promontory Fort	Excavation	AX57	4 slingstones from large heap	stone
93	NMW	Goldcliff	Excavation	98.24H	IA timber posts	wood
94	NPT	Goldcliff	Excavation	90.109	boat plank	wood
95	NMW	Harding Down	Excavation	84.31/1	IA pottery	pottery
96	PA	Hatterall Hill Cwmyoy	chance find	2001 118.2	glass bead blue, found near burning	bead
97	SWS	Knave Promontory Fort	Excavation	A938.42. 1-29	(17) daub fragment	daub
98	SWS	Knave Promontory Fort	Excavation	A938.42. 1-29	(1-16) pottery fragments IA B Ware;	pottery
99	SWS	Knave Promontory Fort	Excavation	A952.12.1-19	(18-19) pebbles, sandstone and conglomerate	stone
100	SWS	Knave Promontory Fort	Excavation		slingstones	stone
101	NMW	Lesser Garth	Hoard	65.82.1	cast bronze terret ring	terret
102	NMW	Lesser Garth	Hoard	65.82.10	coiled terminal of the tang of an iron single-edged knife	knife
103	NMW	Lesser Garth	Hoard	65.82.11	corroded remains of an iron ring	iron
104	NMW	Lesser Garth	Hoard	65.82.2	fragmentary iron bridle bit	bridle
105	NMW	Lesser Garth	Hoard	65.82.3	iron ring with staple attached	iron
106	NMW	Lesser Garth	Hoard	65.82.4	iron lynch pin	iron
107	NMW	Lesser Garth	Hoard	65.82.5	iron ring attached to the expanding and looped end of an iron strip	iron
108	NMW	Lesser Garth	Hoard	65.82.6	iron single edged knife	knife
109	NMW	Lesser Garth	Hoard	65.82.7	iron chisel	chisel
110	NMW	Lesser Garth	Hoard	65.82.8	tapering iron billet	iron
111	NMW	Lesser Garth	Hoard	65.82.9	section of curving iron bar	iron
112	NMW	Lesser Garth	Hoard	93.35H/1 replica	LIA knife handle	knife
113	NMW	Lesser Garth	Hoard	93.35H/2 replica	LIA cauldron ring	cauldron
114	NMW	Lesser Garth	Hoard	93.35H/3 replica	LIA bridle bit	bridle
115	NMW	Lesser Garth	Hoard	93.35H/4 replica	LIA knife	knife
116	NMW	Lesser Garth	Hoard	93.35H/5 replica	LIA latch lifter	iron
117	NMW	Lesser Garth	Hoard	93.35H/6 replica	LIA cauldron ring	cauldron
118	NMW	Lesser Garth	Hoard	93.35H/7 replica	LIA lynch pin	lynch pin
119	PA	Llanmelin hillfort	Excavation	2000.17.1	Celtic coin	coin
120	NMW	Llanmelin hillfort	Excavation	31.345/1(i)	pennanular brooch	brooch

	A	B	C	D	E	G
121	NPT	Llanmelin hillfort	Excavation	77.1	sherd decorated pottery	pottery
122	NMW	Llanmelin hillfort	Excavation	31.30.1	IA pottery and other material	pottery
123	NMW	Llanmelin hillfort	Excavation	31.30.10	fragmentary vessels of IA B from main camp	pottery
124	NMW	Llanmelin hillfort	Excavation	31.30.11	pottery	pottery
125	NMW	Llanmelin hillfort	Excavation	31.30.12	pottery	pottery
126	NMW	Llanmelin hillfort	Excavation	31.30.13	pottery	pottery
127	NMW	Llanmelin hillfort	Excavation	31.30.14	pottery	pottery
128	NMW	Llanmelin hillfort	Excavation	31.30.15	iron slag from annexe of enclosure B	slag
129	NMW	Llanmelin hillfort	Excavation	31.30.16	fragmentary vessels of IA B from enclosure A	pottery
130	NMW	Llanmelin hillfort	Excavation	31.30.17	pottery	pottery
131	NMW	Llanmelin hillfort	Excavation	31.30.18	fragmentary vessels of IA B	pottery
132	NMW	Llanmelin hillfort	Excavation	31.30.19	pottery	pottery
133	NMW	Llanmelin hillfort	Excavation	31.30.2	IA pottery and other material	pottery
134	NMW	Llanmelin hillfort	Excavation	31.30.20	pottery	pottery
135	NMW	Llanmelin hillfort	Excavation	31.30.21	pottery	pottery
136	NMW	Llanmelin hillfort	Excavation	31.30.3	IA pottery and other material	pottery
137	NMW	Llanmelin hillfort	Excavation	31.30.4	IA pottery and other material	pottery
138	NMW	Llanmelin hillfort	Excavation	31.30.5	IA pottery and other material	pottery
139	NMW	Llanmelin hillfort	Excavation	31.30.6	IA pottery and other material	pottery
140	NMW	Llanmelin hillfort	Excavation	31.30.7	cooking pot restored IA B tradition	pottery
141	NMW	Llanmelin hillfort	Excavation	31.30.8	fragmentary vessels of IA B	pottery
142	NMW	Llanmelin hillfort	Excavation	31.30.9	fragmentary vessels of IA B	pottery
143	NMW	Llanmelin hillfort	Excavation	31.345.1	pottery	pottery
144	NMW	Llanmelin hillfort	Excavation	31.345.10	pottery	pottery
145	NMW	Llanmelin hillfort	Excavation	31.345.11	pottery	pottery
146	NMW	Llanmelin hillfort	Excavation	31.345.12	potsherd from flower pot	pottery
147	NMW	Llanmelin hillfort	Excavation	31.345.13	potsherd from flower pot	pottery
148	NMW	Llanmelin hillfort	Excavation	31.345.14	potsherd from flower pot	pottery
149	NMW	Llanmelin hillfort	Excavation	31.345.15	potsherd from flower pot	pottery
150	NMW	Llanmelin hillfort	Excavation	31.345.16	piece resembles plastic	unknown
151	NMW	Llanmelin hillfort	Excavation	31.345.17	2 bronze fragments of bracelet	bracelet
152	NMW	Llanmelin hillfort	Excavation	31.345.18	potsherd from flower pot	pottery
153	NMW	Llanmelin hillfort	Excavation	31.345.19	potsherd from flower pot	pottery
154	NMW	Llanmelin hillfort	Excavation	31.345.2	pottery	pottery
155	NMW	Llanmelin hillfort	Excavation	31.345.20	potsherd from flower pot	pottery
156	NMW	Llanmelin hillfort	Excavation	31.345.21	potsherd from flower pot	pottery
157	NMW	Llanmelin hillfort	Excavation	31.345.22	potsherd from flower pot	pottery
158	NMW	Llanmelin hillfort	Excavation	31.345.23	potsherd from flower pot	pottery
159	NMW	Llanmelin hillfort	Excavation	31.345.24	potsherd from flower pot	pottery
160	NMW	Llanmelin hillfort	Excavation	31.345.25	potsherd from flower pot	pottery

	A	B	C	D	E	G
161	NMW	Llanmelin hillfort	Excavation	31.345.26	potsherd from flower pot	pottery
162	NMW	Llanmelin hillfort	Excavation	31.345.27	potsherd from flower pot	pottery
163	NMW	Llanmelin hillfort	Excavation	31.345.28	potsherd from flower pot	pottery
164	NMW	Llanmelin hillfort	Excavation	31.345.29	potsherd from flower pot	pottery
165	NMW	Llanmelin hillfort	Excavation	31.345.3	pottery	pottery
166	NMW	Llanmelin hillfort	Excavation	31.345.30	potsherd from flower pot	pottery
167	NMW	Llanmelin hillfort	Excavation	31.345.31	potsherd from flower pot	pottery
168	NMW	Llanmelin hillfort	Excavation	31.345.32	potsherd from flower pot	pottery
169	NMW	Llanmelin hillfort	Excavation	31.345.33	pottery	pottery
170	NMW	Llanmelin hillfort	Excavation	31.345.34	pottery	pottery
171	NMW	Llanmelin hillfort	Excavation	31.345.35	pottery	pottery
172	NMW	Llanmelin hillfort	Excavation	31.345.36	potsherd from flower pot	pottery
173	NMW	Llanmelin hillfort	Excavation	31.345.37	pottery	pottery
174	NMW	Llanmelin hillfort	Excavation	31.345.38	pottery	pottery
175	NMW	Llanmelin hillfort	Excavation	31.345.39	pottery	pottery
176	NMW	Llanmelin hillfort	Excavation	31.345.4	pottery	pottery
177	NMW	Llanmelin hillfort	Excavation	31.345.40	pottery	pottery
178	NMW	Llanmelin hillfort	Excavation	31.345.41	pottery	pottery
179	NMW	Llanmelin hillfort	Excavation	31.345.42	pottery	pottery
180	NMW	Llanmelin hillfort	Excavation	31.345.43	pottery	pottery
181	NMW	Llanmelin hillfort	Excavation	31.345.44	iron tie	iron
182	NMW	Llanmelin hillfort	Excavation	31.345.5	potsherd from flower pot	pottery
183	NMW	Llanmelin hillfort	Excavation	31.345.6	potsherd from flower pot	pottery
184	NMW	Llanmelin hillfort	Excavation	31.345.7	fragment of crucible	crucible
185	NMW	Llanmelin hillfort	Excavation	31.345.8	binding fragment	iron
186	NMW	Llanmelin hillfort	Excavation	31.345.9	potsherd from flower pot	pottery
187	NMW	Llanmelin hillfort	Excavation	32.385.1	pottery	pottery
188	NMW	Llanmelin hillfort	Excavation	32.385.10	pottery	pottery
189	NMW	Llanmelin hillfort	Excavation	32.385.11	pottery	pottery
190	NMW	Llanmelin hillfort	Excavation	32.385.12	pottery	pottery
191	NMW	Llanmelin hillfort	Excavation	32.385.13	pottery	pottery
192	NMW	Llanmelin hillfort	Excavation	32.385.14	pottery	pottery
193	NMW	Llanmelin hillfort	Excavation	32.385.15	pot-sherds of Iron Age B	pottery
194	NMW	Llanmelin hillfort	Excavation	32.385.16	appearance of plastic pieces	unknown
195	NMW	Llanmelin hillfort	Excavation	32.385.17	pottery	pottery
196	NMW	Llanmelin hillfort	Excavation	32.385.18	pottery	pottery
197	NMW	Llanmelin hillfort	Excavation	32.385.19	pottery	pottery
198	NMW	Llanmelin hillfort	Excavation	32.385.2	pottery	pottery
199	NMW	Llanmelin hillfort	Excavation	32.385.20	pottery	pottery
200	NMW	Llanmelin hillfort	Excavation	32.385.21	thin piece of flint with ground and polished surface	flint

	A	B	C	D	E	G
201	NMW	Llanmelin hillfort	Excavation	32.385.22	pottery	pottery
202	NMW	Llanmelin hillfort	Excavation	32.385.23	iron shank	shank
203	NMW	Llanmelin hillfort	Excavation	32.385.24	pottery	pottery
204	NMW	Llanmelin hillfort	Excavation	32.385.25	pottery	pottery
205	NMW	Llanmelin hillfort	Excavation	32.385.26	iron slag	slag
206	NMW	Llanmelin hillfort	Excavation	32.385.27	pottery	pottery
207	NMW	Llanmelin hillfort	Excavation	32.385.28	pottery	pottery
208	NMW	Llanmelin hillfort	Excavation	32.385.29	pottery	pottery
209	NMW	Llanmelin hillfort	Excavation	32.385.3	pottery	pottery
210	NMW	Llanmelin hillfort	Excavation	32.385.30	pottery	pottery
211	NMW	Llanmelin hillfort	Excavation	32.385.31	pottery	pottery
212	NMW	Llanmelin hillfort	Excavation	32.385.32	pottery	pottery
213	NMW	Llanmelin hillfort	Excavation	32.385.33	pottery	pottery
214	NMW	Llanmelin hillfort	Excavation	32.385.34	pottery	pottery
215	NMW	Llanmelin hillfort	Excavation	32.385.35	pottery	pottery
216	NMW	Llanmelin hillfort	Excavation	32.385.36	pottery	pottery
217	NMW	Llanmelin hillfort	Excavation	32.385.37	pottery	pottery
218	NMW	Llanmelin hillfort	Excavation	32.385.38	pottery	pottery
219	NMW	Llanmelin hillfort	Excavation	32.385.39	pottery	pottery
220	NMW	Llanmelin hillfort	Excavation	32.385.4	pottery	pottery
221	NMW	Llanmelin hillfort	Excavation	32.385.40	pottery	pottery
222	NMW	Llanmelin hillfort	Excavation	32.385.41	pottery	pottery
223	NMW	Llanmelin hillfort	Excavation	32.385.42	iron slag	slag
224	NMW	Llanmelin hillfort	Excavation	32.385.43	pottery	pottery
225	NMW	Llanmelin hillfort	Excavation	32.385.44	iron slag	slag
226	NMW	Llanmelin hillfort	Excavation	32.385.45	iron slag	slag
227	NMW	Llanmelin hillfort	Excavation	32.385.46	pottery	pottery
228	NMW	Llanmelin hillfort	Excavation	32.385.47	fragment of quartz	quartz
229	NMW	Llanmelin hillfort	Excavation	32.385.48	slingstone	stone
230	NMW	Llanmelin hillfort	Excavation	32.385.5	pottery	pottery
231	NMW	Llanmelin hillfort	Excavation	32.385.6	pottery	pottery
232	NMW	Llanmelin hillfort	Excavation	32.385.7	pottery	pottery
233	NMW	Llanmelin hillfort	Excavation	32.385.8	pottery	pottery
234	NMW	Llanmelin hillfort	Excavation	32.385.9	pottery	pottery
235	NMW	Llyn Fawr	Hoard	12.11.1	bronze looped socketed axe	axe
236	NMW	Llyn Fawr	Hoard	12.11.10	bronze socketed gouge	gouge
237	NMW	Llyn Fawr	Hoard	12.11.11	bronze socketed gouge	gouge
238	NMW	Llyn Fawr	Hoard	12.11.12	bronze razor	razor
239	NMW	Llyn Fawr	Hoard	12.11.13	fragment of socketed axe	axe
240	NMW	Llyn Fawr	Hoard	12.11.14	harness fitting in shape of disc of thin sheet metal	harness

#	A	B	C	D	E	G
241	NMW	Llyn Fawr	Hoard	12.11 15	bronze harness fitting	harness
242	NMW	Llyn Fawr	Hoard	12.11 16	bronze harness fitting	harness
243	NMW	Llyn Fawr	Hoard	12.11 17	winged bronze harness fitting cheek piece	harness
244	NMW	Llyn Fawr	Hoard	12.11 18	fragment of harness fitting winged more than half	harness
245	NMW	Llyn Fawr	Hoard	12.11 19	rectangluar bronze harness fitting	harness
246	NMW	Llyn Fawr	Hoard	12.11.2	bronze looped socketed axe	axe
247	NMW	Llyn Fawr	Hoard	12.11.20	bronze belt hook	belt
248	NMW	Llyn Fawr	Hoard	12.11.21	wrought iron spear head socketed	spear
249	NMW	Llyn Fawr	Hoard	12.11.3	bronze looped socketed axe	axe
250	NMW	Llyn Fawr	Hoard	12.11 4	bronze socketed axe	axe
251	NMW	Llyn Fawr	Hoard	12.11.5	bronze looped socketed axe	axe
252	NMW	Llyn Fawr	Hoard	12.11.6	socketed sickle	sickle
253	NMW	Llyn Fawr	Hoard	12.11.7	socketed sickle	sickle
254	NMW	Llyn Fawr	Hoard	12.11.8	socketed sickle	sickle
255	NMW	Llyn Fawr	Hoard	12.11.9	bronze socketed gouge	gouge
256	NMW	Llyn Fawr	Hoard	13.112	cauldron built up of five tiers of metal overall dia 555 height:352.5	cauldron
257	NMW	Llyn Fawr	Hoard	36.624.1	cauldron overall dia: 560 height: 273	cauldron
258	NMW	Llyn Fawr	Hoard	36.624.2	fragmentary iron sword Hallstatt C part of blade and bone handle plates	sword
259	UWVCN	Lodge Wood	Excavation	none	La Tene II brooch	brooch
260	PA	Lower Machen	chance find	2001 123.32	annular bead (Guido group 5)	bead
261	NPT	Magor	chance find	87 461	LIA pottery	pottery
262	NPT	Magor Pill	Excavation	85.217	(4) base	pottery
263	NPT	Magor Pill	Excavation	85.217.23	horse leg, complete skeleton of, from deep channel to west of 1987 excavation	bone
264	NPT	Magor Pill	Excavation	85.217.24-29	bone and rib bone	bone
265	NPT	Magor Pill	Excavation	85.217.30-51	items 30 to 51 in this collection contain a variety of animal bones	animal
266	NMW	Magor Pill	Excavation	86.55H/1	IA pottery sherds	pottery
267	NPT	Magor Pill	Excavation	94.161.3	body sherds, black shell gritted ware, unworn.	pottery
268	NPT	Margam Beach	chance find	88.48H/1	copper alloy ring headed pin EIA	brooch
269	NMW	Marlborough Grange	chance find	68.311 17	sherds	pottery
270	NMW	Merthyr Mawr	Excavation	01.363.1	four fragments of crucibles	crucible
271	NMW	Merthyr Mawr	Excavation	01.363.2	four fragments of crucibles	crucible
272	NMW	Merthyr Mawr	Excavation	01.363 3	collection of drops and jets from bronze smelting	jet
273	NMW	Merthyr Mawr	Excavation	01.363 4	misc small objects	misc
275	NMW	Merthyr Mawr	Excavation	26.239.1	bronze brooch La Tene 1a	brooch
276	NMW	Merthyr Mawr	Excavation	26.239.10	fragments of crucible with drops of bronze adhered to some	crucible
277	NMW	Merthyr Mawr	Excavation	26.239.11	fragments of crucible with drops of bronze adhered to some	crucible
278	NMW	Merthyr Mawr	Excavation	26.239.12	fragments of crucible with drops of bronze adhered to some	crucible
279	NMW	Merthyr Mawr	Excavation	26.239.13	fragments of crucible with drops of bronze adhered to some	crucible
280	NMW	Merthyr Mawr	Excavation	26.239.14	fragments of crucible with drops of bronze adhered to some	crucible
281	NMW	Merthyr Mawr	Excavation	26.239.15	fragment of iron slag	slag

	A	B	C	D	E	F	G
282	NMW		Merthyr Mawr	Excavation	26.239.16	fragments of folded iron plate	iron
283	NMW		Merthyr Mawr	Excavation	26.239.17	fragments of folded iron plate	iron
284	NMW		Merthyr Mawr	Excavation	26.239.18	fragments of fused bronze	bronze
285	NMW		Merthyr Mawr	Excavation	26.239.19	fragments of fused bronze	bronze
286	NMW		Merthyr Mawr	Excavation	26.239.2	iron ring pin head	brooch
287	NMW		Merthyr Mawr	Excavation	26.239.20	fragments of fused bronze	bronze
288	NMW		Merthyr Mawr	Excavation	26.239.21	fragments of fused bronze	bronze
289	NMW		Merthyr Mawr	Excavation	26.239.22	fragments of fused bronze	bronze
290	NMW		Merthyr Mawr	Excavation	26.239.23	fragments of fused bronze	bronze
291	NMW		Merthyr Mawr	Excavation	26.239.24	fragments of fused bronze	bronze
292	NMW		Merthyr Mawr	Excavation	26.239.25	fragments of fused bronze	bronze
293	NMW		Merthyr Mawr	Excavation	26.239.26	fragmentary strips of bronze plate	bronze
294	NMW		Merthyr Mawr	Excavation	26.239.27	fragmentary strips of bronze plate	bronze
295	NMW		Merthyr Mawr	Excavation	26.239.28	fragments of bronze	bronze
296	NMW		Merthyr Mawr	Excavation	26.239.29	minute bronze nail	bronze
297	NMW		Merthyr Mawr	Excavation	26.239.3	piece of sectioned bronze wire bent into diamond shape	bronze
298	NMW		Merthyr Mawr	Excavation	26.239.30	iron nail	iron
299	NMW		Merthyr Mawr	Excavation	26.239.4	fragments of IA 'B' pottery	pottery
300	NMW		Merthyr Mawr	Excavation	26.239.5	fragments of crucible with drops of bronze adhered to some	crucible
301	NMW		Merthyr Mawr	Excavation	26.239.6	fragments of crucible with drops of bronze adhered to some	crucible
302	NMW		Merthyr Mawr	Excavation	26.239.7	fragments of crucible with drops of bronze adhered to some	crucible
303	NMW		Merthyr Mawr	Excavation	26.239.8	fragments of crucible with drops of bronze adhered to some	crucible
304	NMW		Merthyr Mawr	Excavation	26.239.9	fragments of crucible with drops of bronze adhered to some	crucible
305	NMW		Merthyr Mawr	Excavation	27.380.1	pair of bronze tweezers	tweezers
306	NMW		Merthyr Mawr	Excavation	27.380.2	bronze bar	bronze
307	NMW		Merthyr Mawr	Excavation	27.380.3	fragments of iron ring	ring
308	NMW		Merthyr Mawr	Excavation	27.380.4	three iron nails	iron
309	NMW		Merthyr Mawr	Excavation	27.380.5	bronze round headed pin	brooch
310	NMW		Merthyr Mawr	Excavation	27.380.6	small fragments of folded bronze plate	bronze
311	NMW		Merthyr Mawr	Excavation	27.380.7	fragments of bronze chain	chain
312	NMW		Merthyr Mawr	Excavation	27.380.8	fragments of bronze bent to shape rhomoid	bronze
313	NMW		Merthyr Mawr	Excavation	27.380.9	pottery fragments	pottery
314	NMW		Merthyr Mawr	Excavation	27.66.1	unfinished spindle whorl	spindle
315	NMW		Merthyr Mawr	Excavation	27.66.10	fragment of bronze making crucible	crucible
316	NMW		Merthyr Mawr	Excavation	27.66.11	fragment of bronze making crucible	crucible
317	NMW		Merthyr Mawr	Excavation	27.66.12	fragment of bronze making crucible	crucible
318	NMW		Merthyr Mawr	Excavation	27.66.13	fragment of bronze making crucible	crucible
319	NMW		Merthyr Mawr	Excavation	27.66.14	fragment of bronze making crucible	crucible
320	NMW		Merthyr Mawr	Excavation	27.66.15	fragment of bronze making crucible	crucible
321	NMW		Merthyr Mawr	Excavation	27.66.16	iron fragments	iron

A	B	C	D	E	F	G
322	NMW	Merthyr Mawr	Excavation	27.66.17	numerous jet drops and bronze fragments	jet
323	NMW	Merthyr Mawr	Excavation	27.66.18	fragments of iron slag	slag
324	NMW	Merthyr Mawr	Excavation	27.66.19	animal teeth and bone	animal
325	NMW	Merthyr Mawr	Excavation	27.66.2	frag hand made pottery	pottery
326	NMW	Merthyr Mawr	Excavation	27.66.20	shells	shell
327	NMW	Merthyr Mawr	Excavation	27.66.3	fragment of bronze making crucible	crucible
328	NMW	Merthyr Mawr	Excavation	27.66.4	fragment of bronze making crucible	crucible
329	NMW	Merthyr Mawr	Excavation	27.66.5	fragment of bronze making crucible	crucible
330	NMW	Merthyr Mawr	Excavation	27.66.6	fragment of bronze making crucible	crucible
331	NMW	Merthyr Mawr	Excavation	27.66.7	fragment of bronze making crucible	crucible
332	NMW	Merthyr Mawr	Excavation	27.66.8	fragment of bronze making crucible	crucible
333	NMW	Merthyr Mawr	Excavation	27.66.9	fragment of bronze making crucible	crucible
334	NMW	Merthyr Mawr	Excavation	28.485	bronze ring	ring
335	NMW	Merthyr Mawr	Excavation	29.447	twisted silver wire bracelet	bracelet
336	NMW	Merthyr Mawr	Excavation	35.526	fragments of quern stone	quern
337	NMW	Merthyr Mawr	Excavation	38.656	fragments of pottery	pottery
338	NMW	Merthyr Mawr	Excavation	46.65.1	curved iron knife blade	knife
339	NMW	Merthyr Mawr	Excavation	46.65.2	IA pottery	pottery
340	NMW	Merthyr Mawr	Excavation	47 164.73	fragments of crucible	crucible
341	NMW	Merthyr Mawr	Excavation	47 164.74	bronze fragments	bronze
342	NMW	Merthyr Mawr	Excavation	47.164.75	iron ore	iron
343	NMW	Merthyr Mawr	Excavation	50.466.21	bronze needle	needle
344	NMW	Merthyr Mawr	Excavation	50.466.22	fragment of bronze ring	ring
345	NMW	Merthyr Mawr	Excavation	50.466.23	bronze pin	brooch
346	NMW	Merthyr Mawr	Excavation	50.466.24	misc fragments of bronze objects	misc bronze objects
347	NMW	Merthyr Mawr	Excavation	50.466.25	jets and pearls from bronze founding	jet and pearl
348	NMW	Merthyr Mawr	Excavation	50.466.26	fragments of furnace	furnace
349	NMW	Merthyr Mawr	Excavation	50.466.27	fragment of bronze crucible	crucible
350	NMW	Merthyr Mawr	Excavation	50.466.28	slag	slag
351	NMW	Merthyr Mawr	Excavation	50.466.29	section from handle of hollowed antler	antler
352	NMW	Merthyr Mawr	Excavation	50.466.30	burnt cheek piece of bridle bit	bridle
353	NMW	Merthyr Mawr Warren	chance find	50.466.31	badly corroded iron brooch La Tene I c	brooch
354	NMW	Merthyr Mawr Warren	chance find	50.466.32	badly corroded iron brooch La Tene III	brooch
355	NMW	Merthyr Mawr Warren	chance find	50.466.33	badly corroded iron brooch La Tene III	brooch
356	NMW	Merthyr Mawr	Excavation	50.466.34	misc iron work	iron
357	NMW	Merthyr Mawr	Excavation	50.466.35	violin shaped stone net sinker	stone
358	NMW	Merthyr Mawr	Excavation	50.466.36	fragments of upper part of beehive quern stone	quern
359	NMW	Merthyr Mawr	Excavation	50.466.37	spheroid bead of pale green glass	bead
360	NMW	Merthyr Mawr	Excavation	50.466.38	pot sherds	pottery
361	NMW	Merthyr Mawr	Excavation	50.466.39	plain grey pottery sherds	pottery

	A	B	C	D	E	G
362	NMW	Merthyr Mawr	Excavation	54.19.2	bronze perforated disc with broken shank	disc
363	NMW	Merthyr Mawr	Excavation	54.19.3	bronze perforated disc	disc
364	SWS	Merthyr Mawr	Excavation	A903.11	flint	flint
365	SWS	Merthyr Mawr	Excavation	A903.11	shells	shell
366	SWS	Merthyr Mawr	Excavation	A903.11	114 teeth, shells and flint	teeth
367	SWS	Merthyr Mawr	Excavation	A903.51-8	(1-2) axeheads	axe
368	SWS	Merthyr Mawr	Excavation	A903.51-8	(8) bronze droplets	bronze
369	SWS	Merthyr Mawr	Excavation	A903.51-8	(7) iron scoriae (hearth)	hearth
370	SWS	Merthyr Mawr	Excavation	A903.51-8	(4-5) nails	industrial
371	SWS	Merthyr Mawr	Excavation	A903.51-8	(3) knifes	knife
372	SWS	Merthyr Mawr	Excavation	A903.51-8	(6) iron slag	slag
373	NMW	Merthyr Mawr Warren	chance find	1898.273/22	undated copper alloy metalworking waste	industrial
374	NMW	Merthyr Mawr Warren	chance find	29.208	IA copper alloy bow brooch	brooch
375	NMW	Merthyr Mawr Warren	chance find	38.656	pottery sherd	pottery
376	NMW	Merthyr Mawr Warren	chance find	42.65/2	I A pot sherds	pottery
377	NMW	Merthyr Mawr Warren	chance find	50.466/21	EIA bronze needle	needle
378	NMW	Merthyr Mawr Warren	chance find	50.466/39	plain grey sherd	pottery
379	NMW	Merthyr Mawr Warren	chance find	50.466/4	conical shped (shale ?) button	button
380	NMW	Merthyr Mawr Warren	chance find	58.456/9	flint scrapper	flint
381	NMW	Merthyr Mawr Warren	chance find	58.456/8	IA potsherds	pottery
382	NMW	Merthyr Mawr Warren	chance find	88.205H/1-2	IA potsherd	pottery
383	NMW	Merthyr Mawr Warren	chance find	2000.66H/1	IA potsherd	pottery
384	NMW	Minchin Hole Cave	chance find	2000.66H/2	IA potsherd	pottery
385	NMW	Minchin Hole Cave	Excavation	49.418	quern stone	quern
386	NMW	Mynydd Bychan	Excavation	49.418.1	spiral bronze finger ring	ring
387	NMW	Mynydd Bychan	Excavation	49.418.10	iron ox-goad tip	iron
388	NMW	Mynydd Bychan	Excavation	49.418.11	iron file	iron
389	NMW	Mynydd Bychan	Excavation	49.418.12	fragmentary iron strips and sheeting	strips
390	NMW	Mynydd Bychan	Excavation	49.418.13	IA B pottery	pottery
391	NMW	Mynydd Bychan	Excavation	49.418.14	IA B pottery	pottery
392	NMW	Mynydd Bychan	Excavation	49.418.15	IA B pottery	pottery
393	NMW	Mynydd Bychan	Excavation	49.418.16	IA B pottery	pottery
394	NMW	Mynydd Bychan	Excavation	49.418.17	IA B pottery	pottery
395	NMW	Mynydd Bychan	Excavation	49.418.18	IA B pottery	pottery
396	NMW	Mynydd Bychan	Excavation	49.418.19	IA B pottery	pottery
397	NMW	Mynydd Bychan	Excavation	49.418.2	LIA bronze pennanular brooch	brooch
398	NMW	Mynydd Bychan	Excavation	49.418.20	IA B pottery	pottery
399	NMW	Mynydd Bychan	Excavation	49.418.21	pot shereds from Roman C	pottery
400	NMW	Mynydd Bychan	Excavation	49.418.22	pot shereds from Roman C	pottery
401	NMW	Mynydd Bychan	Excavation	49.418.24	pot shereds from Roman C	pottery

A	B	C	D	E	G
402	NMW	Mynydd Bychan	Excavation	49.418.25	pot shereds from Roman C	pottery
403	NMW	Mynydd Bychan	Excavation	49.418.26	pot shereds from Roman C	pottery
404	NMW	Mynydd Bychan	Excavation	49.418.27	pot sherds from Roman C	pottery
405	NMW	Mynydd Bychan	Excavation	49.418.28	pot sherds from Roman C	pottery
406	NMW	Mynydd Bychan	Excavation	49.418.29	pot shereds from Roman C	pottery
407	NMW	Mynydd Bychan	Excavation	49.418.3	link from bronze chain	chain
408	NMW	Mynydd Bychan	Excavation	49.418.30	pot shereds from Roman C	pottery
409	NMW	Mynydd Bychan	Excavation	49.418.31	pot shereds from Roman C	pottery
410	NMW	Mynydd Bychan	Excavation	49.418.32	pot sherds from Roman C	pottery
411	NMW	Mynydd Bychan	Excavation	49.418.33	pot shereds from Roman C	pottery
412	NMW	Mynydd Bychan	Excavation	49.418.34	pot shereds from Roman C	pottery
413	NMW	Mynydd Bychan	Excavation	49.418.35	pot shereds from Roman C	pottery
414	NMW	Mynydd Bychan	Excavation	49.418.36	pot shereds from Roman C	pottery
415	NMW	Mynydd Bychan	Excavation	49.418.37	pot shereds from Roman C	pottery
416	NMW	Mynydd Bychan	Excavation	49.418.38	fragments of worked bone objects	bone
417	NMW	Mynydd Bychan	Excavation	49.418.39	stone spindle whorls	spindle
418	NMW	Mynydd Bychan	Excavation	49.418.4	iron strip bow brooch	brooch
419	NMW	Mynydd Bychan	Excavation	49.418.40	stone spindle whorls	spindle
420	NMW	Mynydd Bychan	Excavation	49.418.41	stone spindle whorls	spindle
421	NMW	Mynydd Bychan	Excavation	49.418.42	stone spindle whorls	spindle
422	NMW	Mynydd Bychan	Excavation	49.418.43	fragments of beehive rotary quern	quern
423	NMW	Mynydd Bychan	Excavation	49.418.44	fragments of beehive rotary quern	quern
424	NMW	Mynydd Bychan	Excavation	49.418.45	sling stones found with iron ore and slag, human and animal bones and pottery	misc
425	NMW	Mynydd Bychan	Excavation	49.418.5	iron strip bow brooch	brooch
426	NMW	Mynydd Bychan	Excavation	49.418.6	iron catch plate from brooch	brooch
427	NMW	Mynydd Bychan	Excavation	49.418.7	fragments from iron brooches	brooch
428	NMW	Mynydd Bychan	Excavation	49.418.9	iron awl	iron
429	NMW	Mynydd Bychan	Excavation	50.297.1	spiral bronze ring	ring
430	NMW	Mynydd Bychan	Excavation	50.297.2	small fragment of possible iron	iron
431	NMW	Mynydd Bychan	Excavation	50.297.3	fragmentary iron strips and sheeting	strips
432	NMW	Mynydd Bychan	Excavation	50.297 4	pot sherds	pottery
433	NMW	Mynydd Bychan	Excavation	50.297.5	pot sherds	pottery
434	NMW	Mynydd Bychan	Excavation	50.297.6	pot sherds	pottery
435	NMW	Mynydd Bychan	Excavation	50.297.7	pot sherds	pottery
436	NMW	Mynydd Bychan	Excavation	50.297.8	pot sherds	pottery
437	NMW	Mynydd Bychan	Excavation	50.297.9	slingstone	stone
438	NMW	Mynydd Bychan	Excavation	49.418.23	pot shereds from Roman C	pottery
439	NMW	Nash Point	chance find	59.104/1	EIA potsherd	pottery
440	P A	Near Llanmelin hillfort	chance find	99.79.1	human head vessel mount	vessel mount
441	NMW	New Mill Farm	chance find	91.23H/1	IA glass bead	bead

A	B	C	D	E	G
442	NMW	Newton Moor	chance find	97.13H	axe (large) either L/A or BR	axe
443	NPT	nr Chapel Tump	chance find	85.218.6	sherd, combed line decoration	pottery
444	SWS	Oxwich	chance find	A959.4.1-3	(1+2) spearheads	spear
445	SWS	Oxwich	chance find	A959.4.1-3	(3) perforated stone	stone
446	NMW	Penllyn	chance find	97.13H/1	IA socketed looped axe	axe
447	NMW	Penllyn	chance find	97.13H/2	IA/RM iron shaft hole axe	axe
448	PA	Penllyn	chance find	2001.4.1	La Tene 1 brooch	brooch
449	NMW	Penllyn Moor	chance find	97.13H	socketed hooped axe E/A	axe
450	NMW	Penllyn Moor	chance find	49.9	minature copper horse	minature copper horse
451	NMW	Port Talbot	chance find	53.262	rough pillar stone	stone
452	Unknown	Portskewett School	chance find	unknown	La Tene brooch	brooch
453	Unknown	Portskewett School	chance find	unknown	pennanular brooch	brooch
454	NPT	Raglan	chance find	88.141	lynch-pin terminal bronze, holed through side for securing device,	bronze
455	NMW	Rivers Taff & Ely	Hoard	30.130.2	fragment of socketed axe	axe
456	NMW	Rivers Taff & Ely	Hoard	30.130.1	socketed axe	axe
457	NMW	Rivers Taff & Ely	Hoard	30.130.10	triangular razor	razor
458	NMW	Rivers Taff & Ely	Hoard	30.130.11	cap of chariot pole, damaged, bronze	cap of chariot pole
459	NMW	Rivers Taff & Ely	Hoard	30.130.3	socketed chisel socket damaged	chisel
460	NMW	Rivers Taff & Ely	Hoard	30.130.4	socketed chisel complete	chisel
461	NMW	Rivers Taff & Ely	Hoard	30.130.5	socketed chisel	chisel
462	NMW	Rivers Taff & Ely	Hoard	30.130.6	socketed chisel	chisel
463	NMW	Rivers Taff & Ely	Hoard	30.130.7	socketed sickle	sickle
464	NMW	Rivers Taff & Ely	Hoard	30.130.8	part of blade of sickle socketed type	sickle
465	NMW	Rivers Taff & Ely	Hoard	30.130.9	razor of double edged circular type	razor
466	NMW	Rumney Great Wharf	chance find	75.20H/c	IA rim and Roman sherd	pottery
467	NMW	Seven Sisters	Hoard	04.125	bronze terminal rings for three link L/A, bridle bit ring, with red glass	bridle
468	NMW	Seven Sisters	Hoard	04.126	L/A bridle bit ring	bridle
469	NMW	Seven Sisters	Hoard	04.127	L/A terret	terret
470	NMW	Seven Sisters	Hoard	04.128	L/A terret	terret
471	NMW	Seven Sisters	Hoard	04.129	strap ornament consisting of pair of horns with knob terminals	strap
472	NMW	Seven Sisters	Hoard	04.130	ring of sub-circular section	ring sub circular
473	NMW	Seven Sisters	Hoard	04.131	L/A strap union	strap
474	NMW	Seven Sisters	Hoard	04.132	simple buckle	buckle
475	NMW	Seven Sisters	Hoard	04.133	strap ornament	strap
476	NMW	Seven Sisters	Hoard	04.134	silver-plated pendent	pendent - silver
477	NMW	Seven Sisters	Hoard	04.135	triangular connecting piece for straps	strap
478	NMW	Seven Sisters	Hoard	04.136/1	trace hook u-shaped triangular-sectioned bar/inlaid opaque red glass	trace hook
479	NMW	Seven Sisters	Hoard	04.136/2	trace hook u-shaped triangular-sectioned bar/inlaid opaque red glass	trace hook
480	NMW	Seven Sisters	Hoard	04.137/1	trace hook - complete	trace hook
481	NMW	Seven Sisters	Hoard	04.137/2	trace hook - part of pair	trace hook

	A	B	C	D	E	G
482	NMW	Seven Sisters	Hoard	04.138	LIA tankard handle	tankard
483	NMW	Seven Sisters	Hoard	04.139	LIA tankard handle	tankard
484	NMW	Seven Sisters	Hoard	04.140	LIA tankard handle	tankard
485	NMW	Seven Sisters	Hoard	04.141	LIA tankard handle	tankard
486	NMW	Seven Sisters	Hoard	04.142	LIA tankard handle	tankard
487	NMW	Seven Sisters	Hoard	04.143	disc of thin bronze	disc
488	NMW	Seven Sisters	Hoard	04.144	plain round ring	ring plain
489	NMW	Seven Sisters	Hoard	04.145	LIA helmet crest knob	helmet knob crest
490	NMW	Seven Sisters	Hoard	04.146	quadrangular bell	bell
491	NMW	Seven Sisters	Hoard	04.147	circular bell	bell
492	NMW	Seven Sisters	Hoard	04.148	two fragments of lathe turned object - weight 309.8 g	object lathe turned
493	NMW	Seven Sisters	Hoard	04.149	one of two fragments - weight 309.8 g	object lathe turned
494	NMW	Seven Sisters	Hoard	04.150	one of two heavy crescentric or anhor shaped bronze castings	castings
495	NMW	Seven Sisters	Hoard	04.151	one of two heavy crescentric or anhor shaped bronze castings	castings
496	NMW	Seven Sisters	Hoard	04.152	jets from casting	jet
497	NMW	Seven Sisters	Hoard	04.153	jet from casting	jet
498	NMW	Seven Sisters	Hoard	04.154	light chisel	chisel
499	NMW	Seven Sisters	Hoard	04.155	rectangular ingot	ingot
500	NMW	Seven Sisters	Hoard	04.156	thin plated folded into irregular shape	metal plates
501	NMW	Seven Sisters	Hoard	04.157	irregular piece of bronze	bronze
502	NMW	Seven Sisters	Hoard	06.430/1	LIA terret (replica)	terret
503	NMW	Seven Sisters	Hoard	06.430/2	LIA bridle bit ring (replica)	bridle
504	NMW	Seven Sisters	Hoard	06.430/3	LIA strap union (replica)	strap
505	NMW	Seven Sisters	Hoard	06.430/4	LIA tankard handle (replica)	tankard
506	NPT	Seven Sisters	chance find	88.104	lynch-pin bronze with decorated lower terminal or foot	bronze
507	St. Arfon's	Sudbrook	Excavation	34.479	IA quern stone	quern
508	NMW	Sudbrook	Excavation	35.389	knife tang with curved blade	knife
509	NMW	Sudbrook	Excavation	36.438/1	Iron Age c pottery	pottery
510	NMW	Sudbrook	Excavation	36.438/10	Iron Age c pottery	pottery
511	NMW	Sudbrook	Excavation	36.438/11	Iron Age c pottery	pottery
512	NMW	Sudbrook	Excavation	36.438/12	Iron Age c pottery	pottery
513	NMW	Sudbrook	Excavation	36.438/13	Iron Age c pottery	pottery
514	NMW	Sudbrook	Excavation	36.438/15	Iron Age c pottery	pottery
515	NMW	Sudbrook	Excavation	36.438/16	Iron Age c pottery	pottery
516	NMW	Sudbrook	Excavation	36.438/17	Iron Age c pottery	pottery
517	NMW	Sudbrook	Excavation	36.438/18	Iron Age c pottery	pottery
518	NMW	Sudbrook	Excavation	36.438/19	tweezers	tweezers
519	NMW	Sudbrook	Excavation	36.438/2	Iron Age c pottery	pottery
520	NMW	Sudbrook	Excavation	36.438/20	Iron Age c pottery	pottery
521	NMW	Sudbrook	Excavation	36.438/21	Iron Age c pottery	pottery

A	B	C	D	E	G
NMW	Sudbrook	Excavation	36.438/22	Iron Age c pottery	pottery
NMW	Sudbrook	Excavation	36.438/23	Iron Age c pottery	pottery
NMW	Sudbrook	Excavation	36.438/3	Iron Age c pottery	pottery
NMW	Sudbrook	Excavation	36.438/4	Iron Age c pottery	pottery
NMW	Sudbrook	Excavation	36.438/5	Iron Age c pottery	pottery
NMW	Sudbrook	Excavation	36.438/6	Iron Age c pottery	pottery
NMW	Sudbrook	Excavation	36.438/7	Iron Age c pottery	pottery
NMW	Sudbrook	Excavation	36.438/8	Iron Age c pottery	pottery
NMW	Sudbrook	Excavation	36.438/9	Iron Age c pottery	pottery
NMW	Sudbrook	Excavation	99.36H/1	IA pottery	pottery
NMW	Sudbrook	Excavation	99.36H/2	IA pottery	pottery
NMW	Sudbrook	Excavation	99.36H/3	IA pottery	pottery
NMW	Sudbrook	Excavation	35.389.4	copper alloy brooch La Tene III	brooch
NPT	Sudbrook	Excavation	77.8	rim sherd from flat rimmed barrel shaped jar, coarse fabric, EIA	pottery
NMW	Twmbarlwm	chance find	71.12H	spindle whorl	spindle
NPT	Twmbarlwm	chance find	77 13	spindle whorl	spindle
NMW	Twyn y Gaer	Excavation	90.109H/10	sword	sword
NMW	Twyn y Gaer	Excavation	90.109H/12	brooch iron	brooch
NMW	Twyn y Gaer	Excavation	90.109H/14	brooch pin	brooch
NMW	Twyn y Gaer	Excavation	90.109H/15	brooch fragment unknown type	brooch
NMW	Twyn y Gaer	Excavation	90.109H/16	brooch fragment unknown type	brooch
NMW	Twyn y Gaer	Excavation	90.109H/19	iron stud	stud
NMW	Twyn y Gaer	Excavation	90.109H/20	conjoining sherds s/m vessel	pottery
NMW	Twyn y Gaer	Excavation	90.109H/21	knife blade	knife
NMW	Twyn y Gaer	Excavation	90.109H/22	hilt guard	hilt guard
NMW	Twyn y Gaer	Excavation	90.109H/23	1/2 sole shaped iron piece	iron
NMW	Twyn y Gaer	Excavation	90.109H/28	fragment plate sheet	frag sheet plate
NMW	Twyn y Gaer	Excavation	90.109H/29	latch lifter	iron
NMW	Twyn y Gaer	Excavation	90.109H/30	bar with loop made of substantial amoun of iron	iron
NMW	Twyn y Gaer	Excavation	90.109H/31	iron file with markings	iron
NMW	Twyn y Gaer	Excavation	90.109H/32	stripping tool	stripping tool
NMW	Twyn y Gaer	Excavation	90.109H/33	oval ring	oval ring
NMW	Twyn y Gaer	Excavation	90.109H/34	fragment of bracelet iron	bracelet
NMW	Twyn y Gaer	Excavation	90.109H/35	knife blade	knife
NMW	Twyn y Gaer	Excavation	90.109H/7	involuted brooch	brooch
NMW	Twyn y Gaer	Excavation	90.109H/8	possible La Tene 1 brooch	brooch
NMW	Twyn y Gaer	Excavation	90.109H/9	La Tene 2 brooch involuted (arras)	brooch
NMW	Twyn y Gaer	Excavation		brooch pin	brooch
NMW	Twyn y Gaer	Excavation	90.109H6	copper alloy well worked (prestige item)	bronze
NMW	Twyn y Gaer	Excavation	90.110H/10	possible knife blade	knife

A	B	C	D	E	G
562	NMW	Twyn y Gaer	Excavation	90.110H/11	involuted brooch	brooch
563	NMW	Twyn y Gaer	Excavation	90.110H/11	invoiuted brooch	brooch
564	NMW	Twyn y Gaer	Excavation	90.110H/12	involuted brooch	brooch
565	NMW	Twyn y Gaer	Excavation	90.110H/13	involuted brooch	brooch
566	NMW	Twyn y Gaer	Excavation	90.110H/14	cleat	cleat
567	NMW	Twyn y Gaer	Excavation	90.110H/15	iron ring (personal)	ring
568	NMW	Twyn y Gaer	Excavation	90.110H/17	socket or binding pieces with pin	socket or binding
569	NMW	Twyn y Gaer	Excavation	90.110H/2	possible decorated belt fitting	belt
570	NMW	Twyn y Gaer	Excavation	90.110H/20	fragment of brooch	brooch
571	NMW	Twyn y Gaer	Excavation	90.110H/22	bolt	bolt
572	NMW	Twyn y Gaer	Excavation	90.110H/4	spear ferrel butt	spear
573	NMW	Twyn y Gaer	Excavation	90.110H/5	chisel	chisel
574	NMW	Twyn y Gaer	Excavation	90.110H/6	possible involuted brooch	brooch
575	NMW	Twyn y Gaer	Excavation	90.110H/7	fragment of brooch	brooch
576	NMW	Twyn y Gaer	Excavation	90.110H/9	brooch spring	brooch
577	NMW	Twyn y Gaer	Excavation	90.111H/1	fitting of some sort	fitting
578	NMW	Twyn y Gaer	Excavation	90.111H/2	handle	handle
579	NMW	Twyn y Gaer	Excavation	90.111H/4	knife	knife
580	NMW	Twyn y Gaer	Excavation	90.111H/6	iron staple	staple
581	NMW	Twyn y Gaer	Excavation	90.111H/7	possible brooch	brooch
582	NMW	Twyn y Gaer	Excavation	90.111H/8	knife blade	knife
583	NMW	Twyn y Gaer	Excavation	90.111H/9	possible chisel	chisel
584	NMW	Twyn y Gaer	Excavation	90/109H	IA glass bead 1 Of 9	bead
585	NMW	Twyn y Gaer	Excavation	90/109H/2	IA pottery salt container	pottery
586	ABR	Twyn y Gaer	Excavation	unknown	pot-boiler	stone
587	ABR	Twyn y Gaer	Excavation	unknown	sling-stone	stone
588	NMW	Waterstone	chance find	88.10H/16	IA/RM pottery sherd	pottery
589	NMW	Waterstone	chance find	88.10H/17	IA/RM pottery sherd	pottery
590	NMW	Waterstone	chance find	88.10H/18	IA/RM pottery sherd	pottery
591	NMW	Whitchurch	Excavation	59.557	LIA gold spiral ring	ring
592	NMW	Whitton	Excavation	77 40/H - W67BQ	possible pennanular brooches x 2	brooch
593	NMW	Whitton	Excavation	77 40/H - W67IT	possible pennanular brooch	brooch
594	NMW	Whitton	Excavation	W66LX - 10	masons pick	pick
595	NMW	Whitton	Excavation	W66LX - 160	beads glass	bead
596	NMW	Whitton	Excavation	W66LX - 20	bridle bit links	bridle
597	NMW	Whitton	Excavation	W66LX - 21	bridle bit links	bridle
598	NMW	Whitton	Excavation	W66LX - 225	shale bracelet 4 fragments in all (I unpublished)	bracelet
599	NMW	Whitton	Excavation	W66LX - 25	iron pennanular brooch	brooch
600	NMW	Whitton	Excavation	W66LX - 47	metal cross section for holding cauldron	cross section
601	NMW	Whitton	Excavation	W66LX - 5	chisel set	chisel

A	B	C	D	E	G
602	NMW	Whitton	Excavation	77.40h/3	IA iron ingot	ingot
603	NMW	Whitton	Excavation	77.40H/8	IA glass bead	bead
604	PA	unknown	chance find	2000.69.1	human head mount LIA - cooper alloy	mount
605	PA	unknown	chance find	2001.123.46	pelter shaped ingot 9 (similar to seven sisters)	ingot
606	NMW	Woodfield Terrace	chance find	20.319.1	EIA well fired pottery, also flint flake, potboilers	pottery
607	NMW	Woodfield Terrace	chance find	20.319.2	well fired pottery, also flint flake, potboilers	pottery
608	NMW	Woodfield Terrace	chance find	20.319.3	well fired pottery, also flint flake, potboilers	pottery
609	NMW	Woodfield Terrace	chance find	20.319.4	well fired pottery, also flint flake, potboilers	pottery
610	NMW	Woodfield Terrace	chance find	20.319.5	well fired pottery, also flint flake, potboilers	pottery
611	NMW	Worms Head	chance find	24.117.1	valves of a stone mould for bronze ring casting	mould
612	NMW	Worms Head		24.117.2	a ledge	antler
613	NMW	Worms Head		24.117.3	stone disc of volcanic tuff	stone
614	NMW	Worms Head	Excavation	24.117 4	fragment of stone disc	stone
615	NMW	Worms Head	Excavation	24.117.5	spindle whorl	spindle
616	NMW	Worms Head	Excavation	24.117.6	spindle whorl	spindle
617	Unknown	Llancarfan	Excavation	unknown	skeleton	burial
618	Unknown	Llancarfan	Excavation	unknown	scrap of blade	knife
619	Unknown	Llancarfan	Excavation	unknown	iron bar	bar
620	Unknown	Llancarfan	Excavation	unknown	iron bar	bar
621	Unknown	Llancarfan	Excavation	unknown	iron bar	bar
622	Unknown	Llancarfan	Excavation	unknown	iron bar	bar
623	Unknown	Llancarfan	Excavation	unknown	iron plate	plate
624	Unknown	Llancarfan	Excavation	unknown	iron nail	nail
625	Unknown	Llancarfan	Excavation	unknown	two broken nails	nail
626	Unknown	Llancarfan	Excavation	unknown	iron blade- curved	knife
627	Unknown	Llancarfan	Excavation	unknown	iron blade - piece of knife	knife
628	Unknown	Llancarfan	Excavation	unknown	iron blade - piece of knife	knife
629	Unknown	Llancarfan	Excavation	unknown	iron blade - piece of knife	knife
630	Unknown	Llancarfan	Excavation	unknown	iron awl ?	awl
631	Unknown	Llancarfan	Excavation	unknown	iron spike	spike
632	Unknown	Llancarfan	Excavation	unknown	iron strip	strip
633	Unknown	Llancarfan	Excavation	unknown	small iron chisel	chisel
634	Unknown	Llancarfan	Excavation	unknown	iron strip	strip
635	Unknown	Llancarfan	Excavation	unknown	iron strip	strip
636	Unknown	Llancarfan	Excavation	unknown	iron bar	bar
637	Unknown	Llancarfan	Excavation	unknown	iron hook	hook
638	Unknown	Llancarfan	Excavation	unknown	iron stud	stud
639	Unknown	Llancarfan	Excavation	unknown	iron nail	nail
640	Unknown	Llancarfan	Excavation	unknown	iron nail	nail
641	Unknown	Llancarfan	Excavation	unknown	iron nail	nail

	A	B	C	D	E	G
682	Unknown	Caldicot	Excavation	unknown	pennanular brooch	brooch
683	Unknown	Caldicot	Excavation	unknown	pennanular brooch	brooch
684	Unknown	Caldicot	Excavation	unknown	La Tene III brooch fragment	brooch
685	NMW	Sudbrook	Excavation	36.438.14	bronze brooch La Tene III with open catch plate	brooch
686	NMW	Sudbrook	Excavation	34.479	swan-headed pin fragment	brooch
687	Unknown	Sudbrook	Excavation	unknown	bronze brooch with half covered spring of ten coils, five on each side	brooch
688	Unknown	Sudbrook	Excavation	unknown	bronze brooch with covered springs of ten coils, six on one side four on the other	brooch
689	Unknown	Sudbrook	Excavation	unknown	bronze brooch with covered springs of ten coils, five on each side	brooch
690	Unknown	Sudbrook	Excavation	unknown	bronze brooch multi coiled but spring and coil missing	brooch
691	Unknown	Sudbrook	Excavation	unknown	bronze brooch of dolphin type, no hinge pin	brooch
692	Unknown	Sudbrook	Excavation	unknown	fragmentary coiled spring and pin of a bronze brooch	brooch
693	Unknown	Newton Moor	chance find	unknown	La Tene 1Ba brooch	brooch
694						

Bibliography

Alcock, L. 1963. *Dinas Powys: An Iron Age, Dark Age and Early Medieval Settlement in Glamorgan*, Cardiff: University of Wales Press.

Aldhouse Green M, J. 2001. *Dying for the Gods: Human Sacrifice in Iron Age & Roman Europe*, Stroud: Tempus.

Allen, J. R. 1905. 'Find of Late-Celtic Bronze Objects at Seven Sisters, near Neath, Glamorganshire', *Archaeologia Cambrensis*, 6th Series, 5: 127-46.

Allen, D. 1995. *Catalogue of the Celtic coins in the British Museum with supplementary material from other British Collections*, London: British Museum Press.

Arnold C, J and Davies J, L. 2000. (eds). *Roman & Early Medieval Wales*. Stroud: Sutton Publishing.

Avery, M. 1993. *Hillfort Defences of Southern Britain*, Oxford: British Archaeological Reports, British Series 231.

Bayley, J. 1992. *Non-ferrous Metalworking from Coppergate*. York: York Archaeological Trust.

Bayley, J. 1998. Metals and metalworking in the first millennium AD, in Bayley 1998 page number

Bayley, J (ed) 1998. *Science in archaeology: an agenda for the future*, London: English Heritage.

Beck, C and Shennan, S. 1990. *Amber in Prehistoric Britain*. Oxford: Oxbow Monograph 8.

Bell, M. and Parkhouse, J. 2000. *Rectangular structures east of Goldcliff Pill*, In M, Bell, A Caseldine. and H, Neumann. 2000 (eds), pp 83-125

Bell, M, Caseldine, A. and. Neumann, H. 2000. *Prehistoric Intertidal Archaeology in the Welsh Severn Estuary*. CBA Report 120.

Besly, E and MacDonald, P. 2000. ' Lower Llanmelin, Caerwent (ST 45 91)' *Archaeology in Wales* 40, 77.

Boon, G. C. 1974. 'Note', *Proceedings of the Prehistoric Society* 40: 205.

Boon, G. C and Lewis, J, M. (eds) 1976. *Welsh Antiquity: Essays presented to Dr H. N. Savory*, Cardiff: National Museum of Wales: pp. 121-48.

Boon, G. C. 1980. Two iron-age glass beads in the National Museum, *Bulletin of the Board of Celtic Studies* 28, 745-46

Boon, G, C. 1988. 'The Coins', in: D, M. Robinson, (ed). *Biglis, Caldicot & Llandough: There Late Iron Age and Romano-British Sites in South-East Wales: Excavations 1977-79*. Oxford: British Archaeological Report (British Series 188). Pp 91.

Brailsford, J. W. 1975. 'The Polden Hill Hoard, Somerset', *Proceedings of the Prehistoric Society* 41: 222-34.

Brassill, K, S. 1992. 'Ty Tan y Foel, Cerrig-y-Drudion', *Archaeology in Wales* 32: 58.

Brassill, K, S. 1993. 'Ty Tan y Foel, Cerrig-y-Drudion', *Archaeology in Wales* 33: 50.

Brothwell, D and Bourke, J, B. 1995. 'The Human remains from Lindow Moss 1987-8, in Turner and Scaife 1995, 52-29.

Brown, D. 1971. 'A hoard of currency bars from Appleford, Berkshire', *Proceedings of the Prehistoric Society* 37: 326-8.

Bullied, A., and Gray, H. St. G. 1911. *The Glastonbury Lake Village*, I, Taunton.

Burgess, C, B. Coombes, D, G and Davies, D, G. 1972. 'The Broadward Complex and Barbed Spearheads', in Lynch and Cowen 1972, 211-83.

Bushe-Fox, J. P. 1915. *Excavations at Hengistbury Head, Hants in 1911-12*, Society Antiquities of London Research report 3: London.

Carr, G. and Stoddart, S (eds) 2002. *Celts from Antiquity*. Antiquity Paper 2: Cambridge: Antiquity Publications Limited.

Caseldine, A. 1990. *Environmental Archaeology in Wales,* Lampeter: Cadw and St David's University College, Lampeter.

Champion, S. 1995. 'Jewellery and Adornment', In M, J Green (ed). *The Celtic World*, London: Routledge. pp 411-419

Chapman, M. 1992. *The Celts: the construction of a myth*, Basingstoke: Macmillan Press.

Christie, P, M, L. 1978 'The excavation of an iron souterrain and settlement at Carn Euny, Sancreed, Cornwall', *Proceedings of the Prehistoric Society* 44: 309-434.

Clarke, R, R. 1939. 'The Iron Age in Norfolk and Suffolk', *Archaeological Journal* 96: 1-113.

Clarke, S. Bray, J. Davies, J, Leaver, A. Taylor, F. Tuck, M. and J, Wilson. 1999. '*Portskewett, New School development'*, Archaeology in Wales 39: 84-5.

Coles, J and Minnitt, S. 1995. *'Industrious and civilised': the Glastonbury Lake Village*. Taunton: Somerset Levels Projects, Somerset County Council.

Collis, J. 1981. A theoretical study of hillforts, In: G Guilbert (ed). *Hillfort Studies*, Leicester: Leicester University Press.

Collis, J. 1984. *The European Iron Age*. London: Routledge.

Collis, J, R and Champion T, C (eds) 1996.*The Iron Age in Britain and Ireland: Recent Trends*. Southampton: J. R. Collis Publications: Department of Archaeology and Prehistory University of Sheffield.

Corcoran, J.X.W.P. 1952. 'Tankards and Tankard Handles of the British Early Iron Age', *Proceeding of the Prehistoric Society* 18: 85-102.

Cox, P and Woodward, (. 1987. 'The Kimmeridge shale', In Sunter, N and Woodward P, Romano-British Industries in Purbeck, Dorchester, Dorset Natural History Society Monograph 6: 165-72.

Crawford, O. G. S. and Wheeler, R. E. M. 1921. 'The Llynfawr and Other Hoards of the Bronze Age', *Archaeologia* 71: 133-40.

Crew, P. 1986. 'Bryn y Castell hillfort – a late prehistoric iron-working settlement in north west Wales', In: B. G Scott and H. Cleere (eds). *The Crafts of the Blacksmiths*, Belfast: 91-100.

Crew, P. 1989. 'Crawcwellt West excavations, 1986-1989: a late prehistoric upland iron-working settlement', *Archaeology in Wales* 29, 11-16.

Crew, P. 1995. Aspects of iron supply, In B, W Cunliffe (ed). Danebury: an Iron Age hillfort in Hampshire. Vol 6, A hillfort community in perspective, London: Council for research Report 52: pp: 276-284.

Crew, P. and Musson, C, R. 1996. *Snowdonia from the Air*, Penrhyndeudraeth: Snowdonia national Park/RCAHMW.

Crowfoot, G. M. 1945. 'The Bone Gouges of Maiden Castle and Other Sites', *Antiquity* 19: 157-8.

Cunliffe, B, W and Miles, D (eds) 1984. *Aspects of the Iron Age in Central Southern Britain*. Oxford: OUCA Monograph 2.

Cunliffe, B, W. 1984. Danebury. An Iron Age hillfort in Hampshire. York. CBA Research Report 52.

Cunliffe, B, W. 1991. *Iron Age Communities in Britain: An account of England, Scotland and Wales from the Seventh Century BC until the Roman conquest.* 3rd Edition. London: Routledge

Cunliffe, B, W. (ed). 1994. *Prehistoric Europe: An Illustrated History*, Oxford: Oxford University Press.

Cunliffe, B, W. 1994.'Iron Age Societies in Western Europe and Beyond, 800-140 BC', In B, W Cunliffe (ed). *Prehistoric Europe: An Illustrated History*, Oxford: Oxford University Press. Pp: 336-373.

Cunliffe, B, W (ed) 1995. Danebury: an Iron Age hillfort in Hampshire. Vol 6, A hillfort community in perspective, London: Council for research Report 52: pp: 276-284.

Cunliffe, B, W, 1997. *The Ancient Celts.* London: Penguin Books.

Curle, J. 1932. 'An Inventory of Objects of Roman and Provincial Roman origin found on Sites in Scotland not definitely associated with Roman Construction', *Proceedings of the Prehistoric Society of Antiquaries of Scotland* 66: 277-400.

Curwen, E.C. 1948. 'A Bronze Age Cauldron from Sompting, Sussex', *Antiquities Journal 28*:157-63.

Davies, J, L. 1995. 'The early Celts in Wales', In M, J Green (ed). *The Celtic World*, London: Routledge. pp 671-702.

Davies, D, G. 1967. 'The Guilsfield Hoard: a reconsideration', *Antiquities Journal* 47: 95-108.

Davies, J, L. 1973. 'An Excavation at the Bulwalks, Porthkerry, Glamorgan, 1968' *Archaeologia Cambrensis* 122: 85-98

Davies, J, L. & Spratling, M. 1976. 'The Seven Sisters Hoard: A centenary study', In: G. C. Boon and J. M. Lewis (eds). *Welsh Antiquity: Essays presented to Dr H. N. Savory*, Cardiff: National Museum of Wales: pp 121-48.

Davies, J. L and Lynch, F. 2000. The Late Bronze Age and Iron Age. In: F Lynch, S Aldhouse-Green and J, L Davies (eds). *Prehistoric Wales.* Stroud: Sutton Publishing.

Davies, J, L. 2000a. 'The Era of pre-Flavian Campaigning, AD 48-69, In C, J Arnold and J, L Davies (eds). *Roman & Early Medieval Wales.* Stroud: Sutton Publishing.

Dent, J, S. 1982. 'Cemeteries and settlement patterns of the Iron Age Yorkshire Wolds', *Proceedings of the Prehistoric Society* 48: 437-57.

Dungworth, D, B. 1996. The Production of Copper Alloys in Iron Age Britain, *Proceeding of the Prehistoric Society* 62: 399-421.

Dunning, G. C. 1934. 'The Swan's-Neck and Ring-Headed Pins of the Early Iron Age in Britain', *The Archaeological Journal XCI*, 269-295.

Earwood, C. 1991.Two Early Historic bog butter containers, *Proceedings of the Society of Antiquaries of Scotland* 121: 231-240.

Earwood, C. 1993. *Domestic Wooden Artefacts in Britain and Ireland from Neolithic to Viking times.* Exeter: University of Exeter Press.

Ehrenreich, R. M. 1994. Iron Working in Iron Age Wessex, In: A, P Fitzpatrick and E Morris (eds). *The Iron Age in Wessex: Recent work.* Salisbury: Association Française D'Etude de L'Age du Fer/Trust for Wessex Archaeology.

Evans, C. 1989.'Perishable and Worldly Goods – Artifact Decoration and Classification in the Light of Wetlands Research, *Oxford Journal of Archaeology*, Vol 8: 179-201.

Fell, V. 1997. Iron Age Files from England: *Oxford Journal of Archaeology* 16, 79-93.

Fell, V. 1998.Iron Age Ferrous hammerheads from Britain: *Oxford Journal of Archaeology* 17,207-225.

Field, N. 1983. Fiskerton, Lincolnshire, *Proceedings of the Prehistoric Society* 49, 392

Figgis, N, P. 2000. *Welsh Prehistory: Catalogue of accessions in the county and local museums of Wales and other collections*, Powys: Atelier Productions.

Fitzpatrick, A, P and Morris, E, L (eds) 1994. *The Iron Age in Wessex: Recent work.* Salisbury: Association Française D'Etude de L'Age du Fer/Trust for Wessex Archaeology.

Foster, J. 1980. *The Iron Age Moulds from Gussage All Saints.* London: British Museum Occasional Paper 12.

Fowler, E. 1960. 'The Origins and Development of the Pennanular Brooch in Europe', *Proceedings of the Prehistoric Society* *26*, 149-77.

Fox , C. 1927. 'A Settlement of The Early Iron Age (La Tene I Sub-Period) on Merthyr Mawr Warren, *Archaeologia Cambrensis* 82: 44-66

Fox, C. 1929. 'A La Tène I Brooch from Merthyr Mawr, Glamorgan' *Archaeologia Cambrensis* 84: 146-7

Fox, C. 1946. *A Find of the early Iron Age from Llyn Cerrig Bach, Anglesey*, Cardiff.

Fox, C. 1958. *Patterns and Purpose: a survey of Early Celtic Art in Britain*, Cardiff: National Museum of Wales.

Frey, O, H. 1991. 'The Formation of La Tène Culture in the Fifth Century B.C', In S Moscati, V Kruta, O Frey, B Rafftery and Szabo, M. *The Celts*, London: Hudson & Thames. pp 135-65

Frey, O, H. 1991. ''Celtic Princes' in the Sixth Century BC, In S Moscati, V Kruta, O Frey, B Rafftery and Szabo, M. *The Celts*, London: Hudson & Thames. pp 80-103.

Gardner, W. 1935. 'The Bulwalks: A Promontory Fort at Porthkerry, Glamorganshire, *Archaeologia Cambrensis* XC: 135-140

Gent, H. 1983. Centralised storage in later prehistoric Britain. *Proceedings of the Prehistoric Society* 49: 243-268.

Green, M. J. 1986. *The Gods of the Celts*, Gloucester: Alan Sutton,.

Green, M, J. (ed). 1994. *The Celtic World*, London: Routledge.

Green, M, J. 1995.'Introduction: Who were the Celts?', In, M, J Green (ed). *The Celtic World*, London: Routledge. Pp 3-7.

Greep, S, J. 1988. 'Worked Bone', in: D, M. Robinson, (ed). *Biglis, Caldicot & Llandough: There Late Iron Age and Romano-British Sites in South-East Wales: Excavations 1977-79*. Oxford: British Archaeological Report (British Series 188). Pp 58

Gray, H. St. G. 1923. 'Archaeological Remains. Ham Hill, South Somerset'. Proceedings of the Somerset *Archaeological Society* 69: 49-53.

Guido, M. 1978. *The Glass Beads of the Prehistoric Periods in Britain and Ireland*. London: Research Report for the Society of Antiquaries London 35.

Guido M. 1999. *The Glass Beads of Anglo-Saxon England c. AD400-700*, Research Report for the Society of Antiquaries London 56.

Guilbert, G. C. 1981. 'Ffridd Faldwyn', *Archaeological Journal* 138: 20-22

Guilbert, G. C. 1976. '*Moel Y Gaer (Rhosesmor) 1972-1973: an area excavation in the interior'*, In D, W. Harding 1976, pp 303-17

Gwilt, A and Haselgrove, C, C (eds) 1997. *Reconstructing Iron Age Societies*. Oxford: Oxbow Monograph 71.

Hallén, Y. 1994. The use of bone and antler at Foshigarry and Bac Mhic Connain, two Iron Age sites on North Uist, Western Isles, *Proceedings of the Society of Antiquaries of Scotland* 124:189-231.

Harding, D, W. 1976. (ed). *Hillforts: later prehistoric earthworks in Britain and Ireland*. London: Academic Press.

Haselgrove, C. 1999. 'The Iron Age', In: J. Hunter and I. Ralston (eds). *The Archaeology of Britain: An introduction from the Upper Palaeolithic to the Industrial Revolution*. London: Routledge.

Haselgrove, C. Armit, I. Champion, T. Creighton, J. Gwilt, A. Hill, J, D. Hunter, F and Woodward, A. 1999. *Understanding the British Iron Age: An Agenda for Action*. Research seminar.

Haselgrove, C. 1997. Iron Age brooch deposition and chronology, In: J. Hill and C Cumberpatch (eds). *Different Iron Ages: Studies on the Iron Age in temperate Europe*, Oxford: British Archaeological Reports (International Series 602), pp. 51-72.

Hattatt, R. 1985. *Iron Age and Roman Brooches: A second selection of brooches from the author's collection.* Oxford: Oxbow Books.

Hattatt, R. 1987. *Iron Age and Roman Brooches: A third selection of brooches from the author's collection.* Oxford: Oxbow Books.

Hattatt, R. 1989. *Ancient Brooches and Other Artefacts: A fourth selection of brooches together with some other antiquities from the author's collection.* Oxford: Oxbow Books.

Hawkes, C.F.C. and Smith, M.A. 1957. 'On Some Buckets and Cauldrons of the Bronze and early Iron Ages: The Nannau, Whigsborough and Heathery Burn buckets, and the Colchester and London cauldrons', *Antiquaries Journal* 37: 131-98.

Hawkes, C. F. C. and Hull, M. R. 1947. *Camulodunum: First Report on the Excavations at Colchester. 1930-1939.* Society of Antiquities London Research Report 14: London.

Henderson, J. 1981. A report on the glass excavated from Meare Village West 1979, In: B, J. Orme, J, M. Coles.A, E. Caseldine and G, N. Bailey (eds). *Meare Village West 1979,* Somerset Levels Papers 7: 55-60.

Heslop, D, H. 1988. The study of beehive querns, *Scottish Archaeological Review* 5: 59-65.

Hill, J. D. 1995. The Pre-Roman Iron Age in Britain and Ireland (ca. 800 B.C. to A.D. 100): An Overview, *Journal of World Prehistory*, Vol 9: No 1: 47-98.

Hill, J. 1995. How should we understand Iron Age societies and Hillforts? A contextual study from Southern Britain, In: J. Hill and C Cumberpatch (eds). *Different Iron Ages: Studies on the Iron Age in temperate Europe*, Oxford: British Archaeological Reports (International Series 602), pp. 45-66.

Hill, J and Cumberpatch, C (eds) 1995. *Different Iron Ages: Studies on the Iron Age in temperate Europe*, Oxford: British Archaeological Reports (International Series 602): pp. 45-66.

Hill, J. D. 1997. 'The end of one body and the beginning of another kind of body? Toilet instruments and 'Romanization', in Gwilt and Haselgrove 1997, .page numbers

Hingley, R. 1990. Iron Age 'Currency Bars': The Archaeological and Social Context, *The Archaeological Journal* 147: 91-117.

Hingley, R. 1997. Iron, ironworking and regeneration: a study of the symbolic meaning of metalworking in Iron Age Britain, in Gwilt and Haselgrove 1997, 9-18.

Hoare, R. Colt. 1825. 'Account of Antiquities found at Hamden Hill with Fragments of British Chariots', *Archaeologia* 21: 39-42.

Hogg, A, H, A. 1973. 'Excavation at Harding's Down Fort, Gower', *Archaeologia Cambrensis* 122, 55-68

Hogg, A, H, A. 1974. 'The Llantwit Major Villa: A Reconsideration of the Evidence', Britannia 5 (1974): 225-50

Hooper, Bari 1984. 'Anatomical Considerations', in: Cunliffe 1984, 463-74

Howell, R and Pollard, J. 2000. 'Caerleon, Lodge Wood Camp' *Archaeology in Wales* 40: 81-3)

Hull, M, R and Hawkes, C, F, C. 1987. *Corpus of Ancient Brooches in Britain by the late Mark Reginald Hull: Pre-Roman Bow Brooches.* Oxford: British Archaeological Report (British Series 168).

Hunter, J and Ralston, I (eds) 1999. *The Archaeology of Britain: An introduction from the Upper Palaeolithic to the Industrial Revolution.* London: Routledge.

Hunter, F. McDonald, J. G. Pollard, A. M. Morris, C. R and Rowlands, C. C. 1993. The scientific identification of archaeological jet-like artefacts, *Archaeometry* 35: 69-89.

Hunter, F. 1997. Iron Age hoarding in Scotland and northern England, In: A Gwilt and C. C Haselgrove, (eds). *Reconstructing Iron Age Societies*. Oxford: Oxbow Monograph 71: pp 108-133.

Hussey, M. S. 1964-66. Final Excavations at the Lesser Garth Cave, Pentyrch, *Reports and Transactions of the Cardiff Naturalists' Society*. Volume XCIII, pp 18-39

Jackson, R. 1985. Cosmetic sets from Late Iron Age and Roman Britain, *Britannia* 16 (XVI) 165-192.

James, S. 1999 *The Atlantic Celts: ancient people or modern invention*? London: British Museum.

James, S. 1993. *Exploring the World of the Celts*. London: Thames & Hudson.

Jarrett, M, G. and Wrathmell, S. 1981. *Whitton: An Iron Age and Roman Farmstead in South Glamorgan*, Cardiff: University of Wales Press.

Jope, E, M. 1953. 'The enamelled brooch from a souterrain in Angus', *Antiquaries Journal* 33: 69-71.

Jope, E, M. 2000. Early Celtic Art in the British Isles. Oxford: Clarendon Press.

Kilbridie-Jones, H, E. 1938. Glass armlets in Britain, *Proceedings of the Society of Antiquaries of Scotland* 72, 366-395

Lawson, A.J. 1988. 'Shale Objects', In: M, G. Jarrett, M, Henig and S, Wrathmell. 1981. *Whitton: An Iron Age and Roman Farmstead in South Glamorgan*, Cardiff: University of Wales Press. pp 225-6.

Lynch F, M. and Cowen, C, B. 1972. (eds). *Prehistoric Man in Wales and the west: Essays in Honour of Lily F. Chitty*, Bath: Adams & Dart.

Lynch, F, Aldhouse-Green, S and Davies J, L. 2000. (eds). *Prehistoric Wales*. Stroud: Sutton Publishing.

MacDonald, P. 2000. 'A Pilot Scheme for the Recording of Portable Antiquities in Wales', *Archaeology in Wales* 40: 44-7.

MacDonald, P. 2000. 'Newton Moor, Penllyn', *Archaeology in Wales* 40: 91-92.

MacDonald, P. 2000. *A Reassessment of the Copper Alloy Artefacts from the Llyn Cerrig Bach, Anglesey Assemblage*. Unpublished Thesis. Cardiff University.

MacGregor, M. 1976. *Early Celtic Art in North Britain: a study of decorative metalwork from the third century B.C. to the third century A.D.* (two volumes). Leicester: University Press.

Mack, R. P. 1975. Coinage of Ancient Britain, 3rd edition London.

Manning, W. H. 1972. 'Ironwork Hoards in Iron Age and Roman Britain', *Britannia* 3: 224-50.

Manning, W.H. and. Scott, I.R. 1988. 'Ironwork', In: M, G. Jarrett, M, Henig and S, Wrathmell. 1981. *Whitton: An Iron Age and Roman Farmstead in South Glamorgan*, Cardiff: University of Wales Press. pp 188-201.

Megaw, J. V. S. 1966. 'A Celtic cult head from Port Talbot, Glamorgan', *Archaeologia Cambrensis* 115: 94-8.

Megaw, R and Megaw, V. 1989. *Early Celtic Art from its beginnings to the Book of Kells*, London: Thames & Hudson.

Morris, E. L. 1994. 'Production and distribution of pottery and salt in Iron Age Britain: a review', *Proceedings of the Prehistoric Society* 60: 371-394.

Morris, E. L. 1994. 'Iron Age Artefact Production and Exchange', In: J. R Collis and T. C Champion (ed). *The Iron Age in Britain and Ireland: Recent Trends*. Southampton: J. R. Collis Publications: Department of Archaeology and Prehistory University of Sheffield.

Musson, C. R. & Northover, J. P. 1989. 'Llanymynach Hillfort, Powys and Shropshire: observations on construction work 1981', *Montgomeryshire Collections* 77: 15-26

Musson, C. R., Britnell, W.J., Northover, J.P & Salter, C. J. 1992. 'Excavations and metal working at Llwyn Bryn-dinas hillfort, Llangedwyn, Clwyd', *Proceedings of the Prehistoric Society* 58: 265-84

Musson, C, R. Britnell, W, J. Northover, P, J. and Slater, C. J. 1992. Excavations and metalworking at Llwyn Bryn-Dinas hillfort, Clwyd. *Proceedings of the Prehistoric Society* 58: 265-283.

Musson, C, R. Britnell, W. J and Smith A, G. 1991. *The Breidden hillfort: A Later Prehistoric Settlement in the Welsh Marches*, London: CBA Research Reports 76

Nash-Williams, V.E. 1932. ' Horse-Trapping from Chepstow, Monmouthshire', *Archaeologia Cambrensis 87*, 393-4.

Nash-Williams, V.E. 1933. 'Notes: A late bronze hoard from Cardiff' *Archaeologia Cambrensis* 88: 299-300.

Nash-Williams, V.E. 1933. 'An early Iron Age hillfort at Llanmelin, near Caerwent, Monmouthshire', *Archaeologia Cambrensis* 88: 232-315.

Nash-Williams, V. E. 1939. 'An early iron Age coastal camp at Sudbrook, near the Severn tunnel, Monmouthshire', *Archaeologia Cambrensis* 94: 42-79.

Northover, J, P. 1984. Iron Age bronze metallurgy in Central Southern England, In: B, W Cunliffe and D Miles (eds). *Aspects of the Iron Age in Central Southern Britain*. Oxford: OUCA Monograph 2.

Northover, J. P. 1987. Copper, silver and gold in the Iron Age, In: E, A Slater and J, O Tate (eds). *Science and Archaeology*, Glasgow 1987. Oxford: British Archaeological Report (British Series 196).

Northover, J. P. 1988. 'The Late Bronze Metalwork: general discussion. In B. W. Cunliffe (ed). *Mount Batten: A Prehistoric and Roman Port*, Oxford University Committee for Archaeology, Monograph No 26. pp 75-85.

O'Connor, B. 1980. *Cross-Channel Relations in the Later Bronze Age*, Oxford: British Archaeological reports International Series 91.

O'Neil, B. H. St. J. 1942. 'Excavations at Ffridd Faldwyn Camp, Montgomery, 1937-39', *Archaeologia Cambrensis* 97: 1-57.

Orme B, J. Coles J, M. Caseldine A, E. and G, N. Bailey. 1981 (eds). *Meare Village West 1979*, Somerset Levels Papers 7: 55-60.

Owen-John, H, S. 1988. 'Llandough: The Rescue excavation of a Multiperiod site near Cardiff, South Glamorgan, In: D, M. Robinson (ed) *Biglis, Caldicot & Llandough: There Late Iron Age and Romano-British Sites in South-East Wales: Excavations 1977-79*. Oxford: British Archaeological Report (British Series 188). Pp 123-178.

Owen-John, H, S. 1988. 'A hill-slope enclosure in Coed y Cymdda, near Wenvoe, south Glamorgan', *Archaeologia Cambrensis* 137, 43-98.

Palk, N. 1984. *Iron Age bridle bits from Britain*. Edinburgh: Edinburgh University Occasional Paper 10.

Parkhouse, J. 1988. 'Excavations at Biglis, South Glamorgan', In: D, M. Robinson (ed). 1988. *Biglis, Caldicot & Llandough: There Late Iron Age and Romano-British Sites in South-East Wales: Excavations 1977-79*. Oxford: British Archaeological Report (British Series 188). Pp:1-64.

Piggott, C, M. 1946. 'The Late Bronze Age Razors of the British Isles', *Proceedings of the Prehistoric Society* 12: 121-41.

Piggott, S. 1950. Swords and Scabbards of the British Early Iron Age, *Proceeding of the Prehistoric Society* 16, 1-28.

Piggott, S. 1953. 'Three Metalwork Hoards of the Roman Period from Southern Scotland, *Proceedings of the Prehistoric Society of Antiquaries of Scotland* 87: 1-50.

Price, J. 1988. 'The Glass', In: M, G. Jarrett, M, Henig and S, Wrathmell. 1981. *Whitton: An Iron Age and Roman Farmstead in South Glamorgan*, Cardiff: University of Wales Press. pp 149-162.

Probert, A. 1976. 'Twyn y Gaer hillfort, Gwent: an interim assessment', In: G. C. Boon and J. M. Lewis (eds). *Welsh Antiquity: Essays presented to Dr H. N. Savory*, Cardiff: National Museum of Wales. pp 105-20.

Renfrew, C. and. Bahn, P. 1996. *Archaeology: Theories Methods and Practice*. London: Thames and Hudson.

RCAHMW, 1956. *An Inventory of the Ancient Monuments in Caernarvonshire. Volume I: East,* London: HMSO.

RCAHMW, 1960. *An Inventory of the Ancient Monuments in Caernarvonshire. Volume II: Central,* London: HMSO.

RCAHMW, 1964. *An Inventory of the Ancient Monuments in Caernarvonshire. Volume III: West,* London: HMSO.

RCAHMW, 1976a. *An Inventory of the Ancient Monuments in Glamorgan. Volume 1 Part 1: The Stone and Bronze Ages,* London: HMSO.

RCAHMW, 1976b. *An Inventory of the Ancient Monuments in Glamorgan.* Volume *1 Part 2: The Iron Age and the Roman Occupation,* London: HMSO.

Richmond, I. A. 1968. *Hod Hill Volume II: Excavations between 1951 and 1958*, London: British Museum.

Robinson, D, M. (ed). 1988. *Biglis, Caldicot & Llandough: There Late Iron Age and Romano-British Sites in South-East Wales: Excavations 1977-79.* Oxford: British Archaeological Report (British Series 188).

Roman Britain Org. Glossary. 2002. www.roman-britain.org/glossary_m.htm

Rutter, J.G. 1948. *Prehistoric Gower: The early Archaeology of west Glamorgan*, Swansea: Welsh Guides.

Savory, H.N. 1952. Note: Bronze Figurine from Abercarn (Mon.*), Bulletin of the Board of Celtic Studies* 15(1), 72-3 & Plate I, Fig. 2

Savory, H, N. 1954. 'The Excavations of an early iron age fortified settlement on Mynydd Bychan, Llysworney (Glam.) 1949-50. Part 1', *Archaeologia Cambrensis* 103: 85-108.

Savory, H. N. 1955. 'The Excavation of an Early Iron Age fortified settlement on Mynydd Bychan, Llysworney (Glam) 1949-50', *Archaeologia Cambrensis* 104: 14-51

Savory, H, N. 1964. 'The Tal y Llyn hoard', *Antiquity* 38: 18-31.

Savory, H, N. 1969. 'The excavation of the Marlborough Grange Barrow, Llanblethian (Glam) 1967', *Archaeologia Cambrensis* 118: 49-72, fig 7.5

Savory, H, H. 1971. *Excavations at Dinorben, 1965-9*, Cardiff: National Museum of Wales.

Savory, H, N. 1974. 'An early Iron Age metalworkers mould from Worm's Head', *Archaeologia Cambrensis* 123: 170-4.

Savory, H. N. 1976. *Guide Catalogue of the Early Iron Age Collections*, Cardiff: National Museum of Wales.

Savory, H. N. 1980. *Guide Catalogue of the Bronze Age Collections*, National Museum of Wales, Cardiff, pp. 58-59

Savory, H. N. 1980. The Early Iron Age in Wales, In: J, A Taylor (ed). *Culture and Environment in Prehistoric Wales*, Oxford: British Archaeological Reports (British Series 76)

Scott, B. G and Cleere, H. 1986. (eds). *The Crafts of the Blacksmiths*, Belfast: Ulster Museum.

Scott, B. G. 1991. *Early Irish Metalworking*. Belfast: Ulster Museum.

Shepard, T. 1941. 'The Parc y Meirch Hoard, St George Parish, Denbighshire', *Archaeologia Cambrensis* 96, 1-10.

Sharples, N. 1991. *Maiden Castle: Excavation and Field Survey 1985-68*, London: English Heritage Archaeological Reports.

Slater, A and Tate, J, O (eds) 1987. *Science and Archaeology*, Glasgow 1987. Oxford: British Archaeological report (British Series 196).

Smith, R. A. 1908-9. 'A Hoard of Metal Work found at Santon Downham, Suffolk', *Proceedings of the Cambridge Antiquarians Society* 13: 146-63.

Smith, R, A. 1918. 'A particular type of Roman bronze Pendent' *Proceedings of the Society of Antiquaries of Scotland* 2nd series xxx (30), 54-63.

Spratling, M, G. 1972. *Southern British decorated bronzes of the late pre-Roman Iron Age*, (Unpublished Ph.D thesis, three volumes), University of London.

Stead, I, M. 1977. 'La Tène Burials between Burton Fleming and Rudston, North Humberside', *Antiquities Journal* 56, 217-26.

Stead, I, M. 1982. 'The Cerrig-y-drudion "hanging bowl"', *Antiquaries Journal* 62: 221-34.

Stead, I, M. 1985. *The Battersea Shield*. London: British Museum Publications.

Stead, I, M. 1991. The Snettisham treasure: excavations in 1990, *Antiquity* 65: 447-465.

Stead, I, M. 1998. *The Salisbury Hoard*. Stroud: Tempus.

Sunter, N. and Woodward, P. J. 1987. *Romano-British Industries in Purbeck*. Dorchester: Dorset Natural History Archaeological Society Monograph 6.

Taylor, J, A. 1980. (ed). *Culture and Environment in Prehistoric Wales*, Oxford: British Archaeological Reports (British Series 76)

Taylor, R, J and Brailsford, J, W. 1985. British Iron Age strap unions, *Proceeding of the Prehistoric Society* 52: 247-272.

Thomas, H. J. 1956-8. 'Roman Discoveries in the Vale of Glamorgan', *Bulletin of the Board of Celtic Studies* 17: 293-6

Tuohy, T. 1999. *Prehistoric Combs of Antler and Bone*. Oxford: British Archaeological Report (British series 285).

Turner R, C and Scaife R, G. 1995. (eds). *Bog Bodies: New Discoveries and New Perspectives*. London: British Museum Press.

Varley, W, J. 1939. 'Old Oswestry hillfort: excavation by W, J. Varley 1939-40' *Archaeologia Cambrensis* 143: 46-91.

Vouga, P. 1923. *La Tène: Monographie de la station publiiée au nom de la commission des fouilles de la Tène* (Leipzig).

Wainwright, G, J. 1967. *Coygan Camp*, Cardiff.

Wainwright, G, J. Spratling M. 1973. The Iron Age settlement of Gussage All Saints, In G. Carr and S. Stoddart (eds) *Celts from Antiquity*. Antiquity Paper 2: Cambridge: Antiquity Publications Limited: pp 187-214

Warner, R, B. 1993. Irish prehistoric Goldwork: a provisional analysis, *Archaeomaterials* 7, 101-113.

Watkins M, J. 1985. 'A La Tene strap-junction from Churchdown, Gloucestershire, *Proceedings of the Prehistoric Society* 51: 319-320.

Webster, J. Henig, M. and Spratling M. 1981. 'Metalwork', In: M, G. Jarrett, M, Henig and S, Wrathmell. 1981. *Whitton: An Iron Age and Roman Farmstead in South Glamorgan*, Cardiff: University of Wales Press. Pp 163-188

Webster, J. 1988. 'Bronze and Silver Objects, In: D, M. Robinson, (ed). *Biglis, Caldicot & Llandough: Three Late Iron Age and Romano-British Sites in South-East Wales: Excavations 1977-79*. Oxford: British Archaeological Report (British Series 188). Pp 53-6.

Wheeler, R. E. M. 1943. *Maiden Castle*, Oxford: University Press (for the Society of Antiquaries).

Whittle, A.W.R. 1989. *'Two Late Bronze Age occupations and an Iron Age channel on the Gwent foreshore'*, Bulletin of the Board of Celtic Studies 36: 200-3.

Williams, A. 1941. 'Excavations at the Knave Promontory Fort, Rhosilli, Glamorgan', *Archaeologia Cambrensis* XCIV, 210-219.

Woodward, A, B. 1997. Size and Style: An Alternative Study of Some Iron Age Pottery, In: A, Gwilt and C, C Haselgrove (eds). *Reconstructing Iron Age Societies*. Oxford: Oxbow Monograph 71: pp. 26-35.

www.ingramcontent.com/pod-product-compliance
Lightning Source LLC
Chambersburg PA
CBHW061302270326
41932CB00029B/3439